Outbound Sales Mastery

Transforming Lives and Businesses

Written by Daniel Carr
Published by Cornell-David Publishing House

Index

Section 1: Introduction to Outbound Sales

Chapter 1: An Overview of Outbound Sales

Welcome to the start of your sales mastery journey! This chapter will earmark your knowledge for an in-depth understanding of outbound sales and why it is an essential skill in the world of modern business. In this immense cosmos of sales and marketing, outbound sales serve as the cornerstone of achieving business growth and success.

Outbound sales refers to the proactive tactic through which sales teams initiate customer engagement by reaching out to potential customers through various mediums, including cold calls, emails, social media marketing, trade shows, or advertising methods.

Transitioning from past strategies that focused mainly on products or services, outbound sales have evolved with the digital era. It is no more about selling a product, but about building customer relations, demonstrating a real understanding of customer needs, and delivering relevant solutions to them. This method no longer focuses on closing the deal, it is instead centered around nurturing relationships that make your potential customers feel appreciated and understood.

Outbound sales revolves around a precise and step-by-step approach:

- **Prospecting:** Involves identifying potential customers or 'leads' who might be interested in your product or service. This involves extensive market research and utilization of various customer databases and LinkedIn for Business, among others.
- **Outreach:** Based on the defined prospective customers, the next step is to establish a mode of contact. This task is executed through cold calls, cold emails, social media, or in-person meetings.
- **Follow-Up:** Possibly one of the most crucial steps in outbound sales is the follow-up. It includes clarifying doubts, providing further information about the product or service, and persuading the potential customer towards a purchase.
- **Closing:** It is the ultimate step of any sales process. With a compelling proposal that aligns with the customer's needs, the sales representative endeavors to close the deal in this stage.

Sales have historically been regarded as an aggressive profession. However, outbound sales, despite involving direct outreach to potential customers, is not about overwhelming prospects into investing in one's product or service. Outbound sales, at its best, emphasizes addressing the needs and queries of customers, making them comfortable with not just the product or service, but also the brand.

There's a common misconception that outbound sales is an intrusive way of marketing, and in turn, building business. While the aggressive telemarketing calls that interrupt your family dinners might have contributed to this image, it is far from the truth. A strategic and well-executed outbound sales strategy is all about connecting with potential customers at their convenience, discussing their needs, and tailoring your services to suit them. It's more about creating a mutually beneficial relationship with customers that lasts beyond a one-time transaction.

One of the many benefits of mastering outbound sales include greater control over sales process and timeline, building targeted customer base, ability to reach out to new markets, and scaling high-frequency campaigns.

By the end of "Outbound Sales Mastery: Transforming Lives and Businesses," you will not just understand the strategic importance of outbound sales but also master the finesse with which you can transform leads into customers and one-time customers into long-term clients. As we delve deeper into the outbound sales world, we'd like you to keep an open mind, consider new strategies, question old processes, and see how this transforms not just your sales numbers, but also your relationship with your customers.

Subsection 1.1: Understanding the Foundations of Outbound Sales

Outbound sales is a proactive and targeted approach that organizations employ to reach potential customers who might be unaware of the company's offerings or aren't actively looking for the solution. It's a traditional sales tactic where the representatives reach out to potential customers, seeking their attention to introduce products or services. In the world of sales, many find outbound sales challenging. However, it can be transformed into a rewarding experience, significantly impacting one's life and business when done right; thus, the need to master this art.

First and foremost, outbound sales are not just about selling a product or service to the potential customers. It's about understanding their needs, offering them the right solution, and eventually establishing a relationship that goes beyond just a seller-buyer interaction. Hence, mastering outbound sales requires a blend of skills, including persistence, creativity, resilience, communication, and most importantly, empathy.

The success of an outbound sales strategy lies in its execution. It involves:

- **Prospecting**: This is the initial stage in the outbound sales process where representatives identify potential leads or customers. Prospects are usually targeted based on a pre-defined set of qualifications or parameters. Prospecting is critical as it sets the tone for the entire sales cycle and requires strategic planning.
- **Outreach**: Post the prospecting stage, representatives reach out to potential customers. Various methods such as cold calling, emailing, social selling, or in-person meetings can be utilized. The objective here is to generate interest and establish the initial connection.
- **Engagement**: After reaching out, representatives engage the potential customers, share more about the offerings, understand their needs or pain points, and demonstrate how they can provide a solution.
- **Closing**: This is the final step where after a series of discussions and negotiations, the deal gets closed. Here, representatives must ensure that potential customers are satisfied with the solution and convinced to buy the product or service.

In a broader context, the outbound sales process is an opportunity to build relationships with potential customers. It allows you to position your business in front of them, emphasize your value proposition, and showcase how your offerings can solve their problems and enhance their lives.

The mastery of outbound sales is an ongoing effort—it involves continuous learning, practice, and most importantly, the ability to adapt to changing customer needs. This book "Outbound Sales Mastery: Transforming Lives and Businesses" is tailored to provide the needed insights and practical tools to become a master at outbound sales. Our focus is to help you refine your strategies, techniques, and skills to be a successful salesperson. The idea is not just to transform your business but also your life, by instilling confidence and resilience that will transcend beyond your professional sphere.

The subsequent sections will dive deep into each of these aspects, including practical tips and strategies for effective prospecting, outreach, engagement, and closing techniques, along with valuable insights on improving communication skills, resilience, creativity, and empathy. Let's embark on this exciting journey to mastery, transformation, and success in outbound sales.

The Essence of Outbound Sales

Outbound sales represent the heart of any business, both small and large scales. They involve services where sales representatives initiate customer interaction proactively. This form of marketing involves salespersons seeking potential clients, unlike inbound sales, where customers seek products independently.

Firstly, it's vital to understand what outbound sales entail before diving into its mastery. Outbound sales are traditional forms of selling involving Cold Calling (unsolicited calls to prospects) and usually rely on a set of predefined scripts. Unlike inbound sales that target potential customers already interested in products or services, outbound sales strategically place products and services before potential clients.

Dynamic World of Outbound Sales

In a rapidly changing business world, the art of outbound sales is also experiencing a transformation. What used to be a domain of cold calls and mass emails is now a world of advanced CRM software and AI chatbots, along with personalized and automated emails.

Salespersons today have a wealth of customer information at their fingertips, enabling them to tailor-make their approach to meet a specific customer's needs. This is essential in the contemporary business landscape where customers crave personalized experiences.

The Necessity of Outbound Sales

A question that might arise at this point is, why is outbound sales necessary? The reason is straightforward - as enchanting as the idea of potential customers streaming into a business independently sounds, it's not always the reality. Competition in nearly every sector today is fierce, thanks to the internet and globalization. Therefore, businesses need to proactively reach out and convince customers to buy their product or engage in their service. This illustrates the importance of outbound sales.

Effective Outbound Sales Strategy

Outbound sales are not about haphazardly reaching out to potential clients. It requires a comprehensive strategy to be effective. An effective outbound sales strategy involves precise audience targeting, personalized messaging, active communication, persistent follow-ups, and dynamic adjustment based on outcomes.

It also encompasses tracking potential customers' behavior, consistent product or service tweaks to meet customer needs, and nurturing customer relationships for repeat business and referrals.

Conclusion

Outbound sales mastery, therefore, involves much more than just mastering sales scripts or pitches. It adopts an intelligent, strategic, personalized, and persistent approach to finding potential customers while reacting effectively to their needs and wants. It practically involves a business or salesperson reaching out to customers, tailoring experiences, and solutions to fit them, and subtly guiding them through the buying journey.

It's about transforming cold leads into long-term, loyal customers. Hence, mastering outbound sales indirectly translates to business growth and success. But, like any masterful skill, it needs in-depth understanding, meticulous strategy, and regular practice, each of which we shall discuss in-depth in the subsequent chapters of this book.

Outbound sales forms the backbone of the contemporary sales industry, and mastering this art can result in a significant transformation in lives and businesses. Every single term and process involved in outbound sales is an essential building block towards success, and we're going to break down these pieces as we flip through the book.

Subsection 1.1: Understanding the Fundamentals of Outbound Sales

Outbound Sales can be effective in transforming lives and businesses if mastered correctly. This subsection will provide a foundational understanding of outbound sales, its importance, and why businesses today should embrace it as a core part of their sales strategy.

What are Outbound Sales?

Outbound sales is the process of sales reps reaching out to prospects and making attempts to convert them into customers. This traditional sales method involves initiating customer interactions through various channels, which might include cold-calling, sending emails, or direct client meetings. In outbound sales, the driving force is the sales team pitching their product or service directly to prospective clients.

Unlike inbound sales, which waits for potential customers to show interest in your product or service, outbound sales is proactive, creating opportunities to attract potential customers based on strategic planning and systematic attempts.

Importance of Outbound Sales

1. **Reach more customers**: Through outbound sales, businesses can proactively reach out to a larger number of potential customers. By targeting specific customer profiles and demographics, outbound sales allow an organization to tap into a larger market.
2. **Increased control over sale timeline**: While inbound marketing relies on prospects becoming aware and interested at their own pace, outbound sales allow

businesses to take control over the sales process timeline.

3. **Targeted strategy**: Outbound sales often involves a very targeted strategy, which means you can reach out to those prospects who are most likely to buy your product or service. This strategy can be based on certain demographics, industries, job functions, or strategic needs.

4. **Brand awareness**: A well-executed outbound sales strategy can help increase brand awareness among potential customers. By reaching out directly to prospects, businesses can ensure their brand is front and center, rather than waiting to be discovered.

The Role of Outbound Sales in Modern Businesses

In the era of digitalisation, many businesses may be inclined to focus solely on inbound marketing strategies. However, a well-defined outbound sales strategy remains an essential part of a holistic business growth initiative. By combining creativity, analytics, and an understanding of the customer's needs, outbound sales can catalyze business growth and improve customer relationships.

Outbound sales can be particularly effective for B2B businesses or industries where the purchasing decisions are complex and require a more personal touch. Regardless of the business type, outbound sales play an integral role in feeding the top of the sales funnel, nurturing leads, and ultimately converting them into loyal customers.

While mastering outbound sales demands a deep level of commitment and strategic planning, the rewards are often worth the investment. As we delve deeper into this book, we will uncover strategies, techniques, and tools that can help you refine your outbound sales skills and transform your business landscape significantly.

Understanding Outbound Sales

The world of sales and marketing is a vast and ever-changing landscape, which includes a multitude of strategies, methodologies, and techniques that pave the way for business transactions. One fundamental method that significantly influences businesses today is the practice of *outbound sales*. This subsection aims to provide a basic understanding of outbound sales – its concept, its importance, and how it can transform lives and businesses towards achieving success.

Outbound sales involve a proactive approach in which sales representatives reach out to potential customers through various channels such as phone calls, emails, events, or social media. Unlike its counterpart, inbound sales where clients organically find and approach your business, outbound sales require a more aggressive tactic as it involves reaching out to prospects who might not be aware of your business or products. This method focuses on pushing the product or service to the market, seeking potential clients, and converting them into actual customers.

Nonetheless, the core to mastering outbound sales lies not in inundating potential customers with relentless messages or phone calls, but rather in strategically crafting personalized and engaging communications that would interest and entice them. To effectively spearhead an outbound sales strategy, it's of utmost importance that sales professionals develop a deep understanding of their target audience, their needs, preferences, behavior, and decision-making processes. When done correctly, outbound sales can be cost-effective and yield high returns, helping businesses to expand their customer base and increase their revenue.

Outbound sales can be a remarkable tool, leaving lasting impacts on businesses and people's lives. This technique allows businesses to tap into a wider market, unlock potential opportunities, and facilitate business growth. For individuals, mastering outbound sales skills can open doors to promising career opportunities. It equips professionals with essential skills such as persistence, resilience, communication, and negotiation skills that are highly transferable and sought-after in many professional arenas.

Moreover, outbound sales offer a unique opportunity to directly engage with customers, thus fostering strong relationships that are instrumental in shaping the fortunes of businesses. It's a method that provides immediate feedback enabling businesses to iterate and improve their products or service offerings. This customer feedback is vital not just in terms of sales strategy, but also for refining future products, building a strong brand, and fostering lasting customer relationships.

Through the succeeding chapters of this book, "Outbound Sales Mastery", we will delve deeper into the nuances of outbound sales. We will explore the various strategies, techniques, challenges, and methods to overcome them. You will discover how outbound sales can be practiced effectively and ethically, creating mutually beneficial partnerships between businesses and their customers.

The road to mastering outbound sales may be challenging, but it's undeniably rewarding. As you embark on this journey, remember to remain resilient, innovative, and customer-focused. Here's to your outbound sales mastery and transforming not just businesses, but also lives for the better!

Section 2: The Fundamentals of Sales Mastery

Subsection 2.1: Understanding the Selling Mindset

Thinking like a sales master is the first revolutionary step you should take when journeying towards outbound sales mastery. One cannot give what they do not have, and as such, understanding the selling mindset provides you with the tools and mental frameworks necessary to excel in the field.

The Customer at the Core

Successful salespeople recognize that the sale isn't about them as individuals; instead, it is about the customer. Hence, the focus should be on providing holistic solutions to the customers' problems. You are not just selling a product or service; you are selling value, benefits, and solutions.

Curiosity & Active Listening

Superlative sales mastery requires a healthy measure of curiosity. It is this curiosity that propels sales persons to genuinely engage with clients, asking probing questions to fully comprehend their needs, desires, and pain points. In tandem with curiosity is the art of active listening. Not merely hearing words, active listening involves absorbing, interpreting, and responding effectively to customers' verbal and non-verbal cues.

Emotional Intelligence (ESI)

Emotionally intelligent salespeople have higher chances of connection and influencing their customers. Having a high ESI means you can identify, process and manage your emotions and more importantly, those of others. In sales situations, emotional intelligence translates to empathy and the ability to get your customer's perspective – a valuable asset in sales conversion.

Resilience & Tenacity

The sales field can be tumultuous, filled with rejection and discouragement. Having a resilient mindset sets winners apart in this industry. Resilience is your ability to bounce back from setbacks and continue in the face of disappointment. Closely related to resilience is tenacity, the sheer determination and stubborn defiance in the face of challenges; the refusal to give up until the sale is made.

Continuous Learning & Adaptability

The world around us is constantly changing, and so is the field of sales. Successful salespeople understand that learning is an ongoing process, and they embrace opportunities to expand their knowledge base. It is important to stay up-to-date with new sales techniques, technologies, and industry changes. Adaptability is the capacity to adjust one's approach based on these changes, and this flexibility often results in increased effectiveness.

Understanding these components of the selling mindset offers a cornerstone foundation as you construct your outbound sales mastery edifice. They are fundamental attributes to be cultivated and honed for success in any sales-related endeavor. By tapping into these mental frameworks, you gear up to transform not just your sales career but also the businesses and lives of those you encounter in the process. Remember, true sales mastery is not an overnight affair; it essentially stems from continuous growth and the relentless pursuit of excellence.

Subsection 2.1: Understanding the Concept of Outbound Sales

Before embarking on the journey to mastering outbound sales, it is crucial to grasp the core concept behind this fundamental promotional strategy in business. Outbound sales can be succinctly defined as a traditional sales strategy where salespeople reach out to potential customers to persuade them to purchase their company's products or services. These tactics often employ methods like direct mails, telemarketing calls, trade shows, and television or radio commercials to attract potential customers.

In the advent of digitalization, new media platforms like social media marketing, email marketing, and pay-per-click (PPC) advertising are also effectively used. They encompass generating leads, pitching sales, negotiating contracts, and closing deals with clients. It differs significantly from inbound sales, which rely on organic methods to attract customers, such as content marketing, search engine optimization (SEO), website design, and other strategies that draw customers actively seeking products or services to your platform.

Subsection 2.1.1: The Art of Outbound Sales Prospecting

The first step in outbound sales involves identifying potential customers to engage with, commonly known as prospecting. Sales prospecting involves conducting thorough research to locate individuals who could be ideal potential clients for what your business is offering.

The prospects could be anyone, depending on the nature of your business—from small vendors to big corporates who may gain value from your products and services. The crucial left task to the sales team would be to develop tailor-fit propositions and connect with these prospects to convince them about the benefits of their company's products or services.

Subsection 2.2: Mastering the Outbound Sales Process

Achieving excellence in outbound sales is a meticulous process. It requires comprehensive knowledge about your products, the market, client needs, and persuasive communication skills. A practical and effective outbound sales process typically involves steps like;

- **Preparation:** This includes exhaustive lead and market research and crafting personalized and convincing sales pitches.
- **Initial Contact:** The next step is making the initial contact with the potential customers with well-framed, persuasive messages.
- **Follow-Up:** This step is crucial as most sales are often made in follow-ups. Persistence is key here.
- **Assessment:** Understanding client needs and assessing the best ways your product can help solve their problem or needs.

- **Presentation:** Here, you create and deliver tailored presentations or demonstrations that highlight the benefits of your product to the prospect.
- **Objection Handling:** Addressing any resistance or concerns your prospects may have.
- **Closing the Sale:** Finalizing the deal by getting the client's confirmation to buy.
- **After-Sales Service:** The business-customer relationship does not end once the purchase is made. Providing excellent post-sale service creates an opportunity for further business and referrals.

Subsection 2.3: Essential Skills to Master Outbound Sales

Succeeding in outbound sales requires mastery over specific skills that go beyond product knowledge and a high degree of enthusiasm. Some of the essential skills include;

- **Interpersonal Skills:** Strong relationship-building capabilities to build trust and credibility.
- **Communication Skills:** Ability to convey and articulate your thoughts effectively.
- **Listening Skills:** Understanding the client's needs is as important as pitching the sales.
- **Negotiation Skills:** In sales, negotiation can often mean the difference between a deal and a missed opportunity.
- **Resilience:** Facing rejections is a part and parcel of the process, and not letting that affect the morale is crucial to keep going.
- **Analytical Skills:** Requisite to assess the market trends and consumer behavior.

Remember, outbound sales mastery is as much a science as it is an art. It takes time to perfect, but with persistent efforts and the above-mentioned strategies, achieving outbound sales excellence becomes an attainable feat!

Chapter 6 : Understanding the Buyer's Journey

In mastering outbound sales, it is critical to understand your timeline and process. The timeline revolves around the buyer's journey - the process your potential customer goes through from recognizing they have a problem, to considering potential solutions, to making the decision to purchase.

Stages of the Buyer's Journey

1. Awareness Stage

This is when the buyer realizes they have a problem. In this stage, the buyer has only developed symptom recognition, but hasn't yet defined exactly what the problem is. As a salesperson, your job is to help crystallize those symptoms into a tangible problem. Through engaging content, thought leadership and strategic outreach you can help your prospect articulate their challenges.

2. Consideration Stage

At this point, the buyer clearly understands and articulates their problem or opportunity. They are now committed to researching and understanding all available approaches or methods to solving the identified problem. It's pivotal to position your solution as the best fit at this stage. You want to demonstrate both domain expertise in handling such challenges, and clearly specify why your product or service is superior to others on the market.

3. Decision Stage

The decision stage is the final one where the buyer has now decided on a solution category. They already have a list of potential vendors and are in the process of comparing offerings before they make a purchase decision. Here, your task is to ensure your product stands out above the competition. You can do this through case studies, testimonials, and demonstrations of your product's value proposition.

Understanding the Buyer's Needs

To effectively guide your buyer through these stages, empathetic comprehension of their needs is essential. By paying close attention to the verbal and non-verbal cues, you can tailor your approach and messaging to meet those needs. It is not about hard selling, but about genuinely wanting to solve the customer's problem.

Aligning Sales Process with the Buyer's Journey

In outbound sales mastery, your sales process should orient around your buyer's journey. Each step in your sales posture must match the buyer's progression through the awareness, consideration and decision stages. This alignment not only increases your chances of closing deals, but also fosters trust with your potential customers.

Objection Handling in the Buyer's Journey

Objections are commonplace in any sales process. However, they often point to gaps in the buyer's understanding of their problem, solution or your product. Therefore, instead of perceiving objections as obstacles, see them as opportunities to provide clarity and build credibility. Skillful objection handling involves listening, understanding, empathizing and then responding.

By understanding the buyer's journey, you can anticipate possible objections at each stage and be prepared to deal with them effectively.

Remember, mastery in outbound sales doesn't only revolve around your product knowledge, or your sales skills, but significantly depends on your understanding of the buyer's journey. The ability to effectively guide your potential customer through each stage of the journey, addressing their needs and predilections, ultimately sets you apart in the competitive world of sales.

Chapter 6: Understanding Your Product and Your Market

The key to successful selling lies not just in your abilities as a salesperson, but critically how deeply you understand both the product you are selling and the market you are selling to. Mastery in sales is not magic—it is a blend of research, knowledge, strategy, and relationship-building. Without an in-depth understanding of your product and your market, you won't have a solid foundation for your outbound sales strategies.

Subsection 6.1: Master Your Product

The product is the Heart of any sales process. Understanding the ins and outs of your product is much more than just familiarizing yourself with its features or specifications. It's about knowing what problems it solves, understanding its benefits, and knowing how it stacks up against the competition.

Walk in Your Customers' Shoes: Your customers are buying solutions to problems, not just products. Therefore, it's essential to understand your product's functionality from the user's perspective. Spending time using your product can get you this vital point of view. Know the product so well that you can discuss it accurately and passionately.

Value Proposition: Clearly identify and understand your product's unique value proposition—what sets it above and beyond the competition? This is what you'll be focusing on when you pronounce your sales pitch.

Competitor Analysis: In knowing your product, you must also be aware of what your competitors are offering. By understanding how your product distinguishes itself from others in the market, you can better communicate these differences to potential clients.

Subsection 6.2: Decode Your Market

The market horizon is vast, constantly evolving, and highly competitive. Understanding your market requires a comprehensive insight into your customer profile, the current market trends, competitive landscape, and pertinent regulatory or economic factors affecting your product's sales success. Keep a pulse on what's happening in your industry, and keep tabs on what your competitors are doing.

Identify your Ideal Client Profile: Getting to know who your potential customers are will enable you to tailor your outbound sales messaging. Understand their needs, challenges, pain points, and preferences.

Understand Market Dynamics: Stay updated with market trends and economic indicators relevant to your industry. These can considerably impact how you position your product and pitch to potential clients.

Customer Behavior: Analyze how customers are interacting with your product, what features they are utilizing the most, which aspects they like or don't like. This will give you a deeper understanding of your customers' needs and how you can tailor your messaging to meet these needs.

Consider Cultural Factors: It's also essential to understand the cultural aspects that might affect your sales, especially if you're selling to a global market. In such cases, knowing the local languages, customs, business practices, and regulations is crucial.

In conclusion, mastering your product and understanding your market are interconnected. They form the primary foundations upon which all your outbound sales strategies are built. The deeper your insight into your product and market, the more effective you'll be in connecting with prospective clients, addressing their needs and, ultimately, closing sales deals. Through continuous learning and adapting, you can genuinely transform your sales game and, in turn, your life and your business.

Subsection 2.1: Understanding Your Audience

In mastering outbound sales, understanding your target audience's needs, wants, and pain points forms the springboard. Creating a buyer persona is more than just recognizing who your potential clients are; it involves a deep understanding of their goals, challenges, and lifestyle.

To get inside the heads of your potential clients, you need to be asking the right questions. The following are some of the key things you need to understand about your target audience:

- *Who are they?* Start with basic demographics like age, gender, location, and job title. What industries do they operate in? What is their role in the organization?
- *What do they want?* What are their objectives and aspirations both professionally and personally? Can your product or service be a vehicle helping them achieve their goals?
- *What are their challenges?* Understanding their problem areas permits you to comprehend how your product or service can resolve these issues. It allows you to position your offering as a solution.
- *Where do they consume content?* Find out whether they spend time on specific social media platforms, subscribe to certain publications, or attend specified conferences. Knowing where your audience obtains their information can form an integral part of your outreach strategy.
- *What is their purchasing process?* Get an insight of how they make decisions. Who is involved in the decision-making process, how long do they typically take to make a decision, and what factors influence their choices?

Developing a granular understanding of your target client enables you to personalize your outreach efforts and establish a resonating connection. Use this knowledge not only to approach the right people but also to craft compelling and personalized messages that pique your prospect's interest.

Subsection 2.2: Crafting a Winning Value Proposition

Your value proposition is a succinct explanation of why a customer should choose you over your competitors. In simpler terms, it refers to the unique value that you promise to deliver to your customers if they choose your product or service.

Here are some steps to createa compelling value proposition:

- *Identify Customer Pain Points:* Draw insights from your understanding of the target audience and outline what problems your buyer persona is trying to solve.
- *Present Your Solution:* This is your product or service. Describe how it addresses the pain points identified above. Remember to focus on benefits, not features.
- *Highlight Unique Differentiators:* Delineate what makes your product or service stand out from the competition. Use this as an opportunity to express why your solution is the best fit for your customers.
- *Communicate the Outcome:* Help potential clients envision the positive outcomes or results from using your product or service.

Remember, your value proposition must be clear, concise, and compelling. It should capture attention, stir interest, and initiate a conversation.

Subsection 2.3: Mastering the Art of Prospecting

Prospecting is an integral part of outbound sales, but it's often overlooked or avoided. Reluctance in prospecting often results from unfamiliarity or fear of rejection. Mastering this art can dramatically influence your sales outcome.

Effective prospecting includes:

- *Research:* Before initiating contact, perform research to understand your prospects and their businesses better. It helps not only in personalizing your outreach efforts but also in predicting their needs.
- *Cold Calling:* Despite the rise of digital technology, cold calling remains a potent prospecting tool in sales. It's all about creating a concise and well-structured pitch highlighting the value your product or service brings.
- *Email Prospecting:* This is essential, especially in B2B sales. An effective email is personalized, succinct, and has a clear call to action.
- *Social Selling:* Use professional networks such as LinkedIn to establish connections, share insights, and engage with potential customers.

The key to successful prospecting lies in staying consistent, persistent, and resilient, while also learning from failures and tweaking your approach when necessary.

Transcending beyond a simple transactional relationship to create genuine connections with your prospects can lead you to master the art of outbound sales. Embrace these fundamental skills to transform not only your sales career but also the lives and businesses of the clients you serve.

Section 3: Essential Sales Tactics & Techniques

3.1 Defining Your Target Market

Identifying your target market is the foundation of an effective outbound sales strategy. It attracts those most likely to need and buy your product or service, which helps streamline your sales efforts and boost conversion rates.

First, make use of `market research` to determine the demographics and psychographics of your ideal customer. Demographic data includes age, gender, location, occupation, socioeconomic status, and any other information that defines who they are as an individual. It's equally important to understand psychographics, which are the lifestyle, attitudes, behaviors, and buying habits of your customers. This will provide deeper insight into what they value and how to best approach them.

Next, consider creating `buyer personas`. These are detailed profiles of your ideal customers. The personas can include data on motivations, pain-points and everything necessary for building an effective sales narrative. Buyer personas can guide your sales outreach communication and enhance your chances of success.

3.2 Crafting a Powerful Sales Pitch

Your sales pitch is a crucial element of the outbound selling process. It's your business's first impression and can greatly influence whether a prospect becomes a customer.

First, you want your pitch to clearly a convey `value proposition`. This statement explains how your product or service solves customers' problems, delivers specific benefits and outlines why they should buy from you and not your competitors.

Next, make sure your pitch is also segmented and `personalized` for each prospect or persona. Grouping similar prospects and tailoring the message to each group can significantly improve response and conversion rates.

The end game of your pitch should be to ignite a `conversation` with the prospect. Encourage them to engage, ask questions and share their needs.

3.3 Mastering the Art of Cold Calling

Cold calling, while deemed as old-fashioned and intrusive by some, can still be an effective outbound sales tactic when done right. Your goal should not be to make a sale on the first call, but rather to build a relationship with the prospect.

To succeed in cold calling, you need to `plan and prepare` ahead. Have a clear understanding of the goal of the call and the needs of the prospect. Your tone of voice and vocabulary play a key role in maintaining the `professionalism` of the call and building trust with the prospect.

Ensure to handle `objections` effectively. View objections as opportunities and use them to provide more information, thereby convincing prospects of your product or service's value proposition.

3.4 Utilizing Email Effectively

Email is a vital tool in an outbound sales strategy as it allows you to reach prospects directly, at scale. Your goal with email should be to pique the interest of your prospects and encourage them to respond.

Ensure your email is clear and concise. Too much information can be confusing and can lead to key points being missed. Use formatting to your advantage to make the email easy to scan and absorb.

Emails should also be personalized and value-focused for the best results. Make the prospect feel that the email was specifically created for them and clearly outline the benefits of your product or services.

Emails often go unreplied to, so it's important to follow up when appropriate. Several follow-ups could be necessary before getting a reply, however, keep in mind not to spam the people you contact.

3.5 Managing and Evaluating Your Outbound Sales Efforts

To ensure the efficiency and success of your outbound sales operation, proper management and evaluation processes must be in place.

Implement a CRM system to handle your sales data. This system can hold valuable insights such as prospect contact details, the status of your outreach, and other relevant information.

Track and measure your sales activities, take note of what's working and what isn't, then optimize accordingly. Important metrics to monitor include call-to-deal ratio, email response rates, conversion rate, and average deal size.

Don't forget the importance of continuous learning and development. Attend seminars, workshops, and trainings to keep up-to-date with the latest trends and techniques in outbound sales.

Each of these tactics and techniques has its own subtleties and nuances. Mastery of outbound sales means understanding and implementing these subtleties effectively. With the right knowledge, tools, and attitude, you can transform lives and businesses through outstanding outbound sales. Stay relentless in your pursuit of sales success, and remember that every bit of effort you invest will get you one step closer to becoming a master of outbound sales.

III.1. Understanding Buying Signals

As an effective outbound sales professional, one of the first and most essential techniques you need to master is the ability to identify buying signals from potential clients. These signs assist you in recognizing when a prospect is ready to move from consideration to purchase. Therefore, understanding these hints can significantly improve your sales conversion rates, transforming lives and businesses.

III.2. Purposeful & Persuasive Communication

Communication is the key to a successful sale, particularly in outbound sales where the initial contact is usually a cold call. The art of persuasive communication revolves around presenting your product or service in a way that resonates with the client's needs and wants, ultimately driving them towards a positive buying decision.

Use purposeful communication to achieve several key objectives: to garner the prospect's attention, build a relationship, discover needs and, finally, close the sale. Be sure to customize your spiel, so it feels personalized and less of a script, leading to increased customer interest and engagement.

III.3. Active Listening

Active listening isn't just about hearing the words spoken by your prospects; it's about understanding the message behind those words. Don't fall into the trap of planning your response while the prospect is still talking. Instead, engage with what is being said, showing interest and understanding. Empathize with their pain points and use this information to tailor your solution.

III.4. Solution Selling

Rather than just pushing your product or service, successful outbound salespeople sell solutions. They identify the issues or pain points businesses are facing and demonstrate how their unique offering can precisely address these problems. Solution selling fosters stronger customer relationships as it proves that you care about their business, not just your own.

III.5. Consistent Follow Ups

Persistence, coupled with politeness, is a powerful tool that can turn a tentative "maybe" into a "yes". A follow-up is a gentle reminder to your prospects that you're there to help address their needs. It shows them you are persistent and committed to offering a solution. However, be careful not to overdo the follow-ups and become a nuisance to the prospect.

III.6. Handling Objections

Objections are an inevitable part of the sales process. Exceptional salespeople anticipate objections and are prepared to address them with evidence, understanding, and patience. Remember, overcoming objections is not about winning an argument; it's about clarifying any concerns or misunderstandings to the satisfaction of the prospect.

III.7. Closing Techniques

Last but not the least is mastering the art of closing the deal. After you've done the work to identify potential clients, communicate effectively, listen actively, propose your solution, follow up consistently, and tackle objections, it's time to close the deal.

There are numerous closing techniques to choose from, and the right one largely depends on the individual transaction. These include the summary close, wherein you recap the features and benefits agreed upon; the assumptive close, where you assume the sale is done and schedule the next steps; and the urgency close, which encourages prospects to make a decision by illustrating what they stand to lose if they delay.

Master these sales tactics and techniques, and you'll be well on your way to achieving outbound sales mastery, transforming not just your business but also your personal life as you grow and improve with each learning experience.

3.1 Mastering the Art of Prospecting

Prospecting is the lifeblood of sales. It's the number one activity that allows salespeople to win new customers and close more deals. Understanding and perfecting this crucial outbound sales tactic can radically transform your businesses by optimizing your sales funnel.

Importance of Prospecting

Prospecting refers to the process of seeking out potential customers who might be interested in your product or service. It involves a range of activities, including cold calling, sending emails, attending trade shows, and leveraging social media to identify potential leads.

While lead generation is typically associated with inbound sales, in outbound sales, prospecting is a proactive process. Rather than relying on incoming leads and waiting for customers to find you, an outbound approach means deliberately seeking out customers who may benefit from what you have to offer.

Building a Prospective Customer Profile

The key to effective prospecting is understanding who your ideal customer is. This candidate, often referred to as your buyer persona, is a detailed profile of the person who will benefit most from your product or service. When crafting this profile, consider factors like:

- Demographics: What's their age, gender, income level, and employment status?
- Industry: What field do they work in? What is their role?
- Challenges: What problems do they face that your product or service could help solve?

Once you have this information, you can use it to guide your prospecting activities, ensuring you're targeting the right people at the right time with the right message.

Multi-channel Prospecting

In today's digital world, there are more ways than ever to reach out to potential customers. Embrace a multi-channel approach to prospecting to increase your chances of making a connection with your target audience. This could involve:

- **Cold Calling:** Despite numerous advancements in technology, there's still a place for this traditional form of outbound sales. The key is taking a tailored, personalized approach that focuses on the prospect's needs, not just pushing your product.
- **Emails:** With over 4 billion users worldwide, email remains a powerful outreach tool for salespersons. Just be sure to personalize your correspondence and provide clear, value-driven content.
- **Social Selling:** LinkedIn, Twitter, Facebook and Instagram offer unique opportunities for salespersons to connect with potential customers. Remember to approach social media as a platform for building relationships, not just sales.
- **Events and Trade Shows:** These offer an opportunity to interact face-to-face with potential customers. You can provide demos, answer questions, and establish a personal connection that can often lead to a sale.

Tracking Prospecting Success

Inbound prospects tend to be more inclined to buy, making them easier to convert. With outbound prospects, the road to conversion can be a longer one. Tracking progression and measuring success are therefore essential.

Consider tracking metrics such as response rates, conversion rates, closed sales, and the average time it takes to convert a prospect. By keeping a close eye on these data points, you can adjust your tactics as necessary to improve your outbound sales success.

Prospecting is not a one-time act. It's an ongoing process that you have to commit to in order to reap the benefits. With a solid understanding of your prospective customer profile, a multi-channel outreach strategy, and robust tracking system, you can excel at outbound sales, and in turn, achieve a profitable business transformation.

3.1 Understanding Your Customers and Their Needs

One of the most integral aspects of outbound sales mastery is understanding your customers and their needs. Before you reach out to your potential customers, it's essential to understand who they are, what they need, and how your product can fulfill their needs. This understanding involves market research, customer analysis, and empathetic communication.

Market Research: This is the starting point of any essential sales tactics. It involves collecting and analyzing information about your targeted market, including details about potential customer needs, preferences, and motivations. Successful market research provides insights into what customers want, thus guiding your sales approach to resonate with potential buyers.

- **Demographic Research:** This form of research focuses on understanding the age, gender, income, lifestyle, and education level of your potential customers. This information is vital to tailor your messages accordingly. For example, if your product or service caters to high-earning professionals, you'll want to use language and messaging that resonates with this group.

- **Psychographic Research:** This research is about understanding the personality, values, attitudes, interests, and lifestyles of your market. This kind of insight makes your messaging more personal and relatable.

- **Behavioral Research:** This involves observing the behaviors of your target audience, i.e., their purchase habits, usage rate, loyalty, etc. Understanding such behaviors aids in creating a sales strategy.

Customer Analysis: After gathering pertinent data about your market, it's time to delve deeper. Customer analysis refers to evaluating customer data in order to identify key subsets of your customers. Each subset possesses unique characteristics and needs. Your aim should be to understand these unique needs and shape your offering accordingly.

- **Identify Customer Pain Points:** These are specific problems that prospective customers of your business are experiencing. Pain points are diverse and vary depending on the target customer and industry. Identifying these help to establish your product as a solution.

- **Identify Customer Goals:** The next step is to understand what your customers are trying to achieve. If you understand what your customers' goals are, you can explain how your product or service can help them achieve those goals.

- **Understand the Buyers' Journey:** Understanding where your customer is in their buying journey (i.e., awareness, consideration, and decision stage) allows you to deliver the right message at the right time.

Empathetic Communication: No matter how well you understand your customers, your outbound sales mastery will fall short if you can't communicate effectively. Empathy is key to building rapport and trust with your potential customers. Empathetic communication isn't just about 'understanding'; it's about showing that understanding to your customers through your communications.

- **Use Active Listening:** This is key to empathetic communication. Reflecting back what the customers say and letting them direct the conversation helps to build rapport.
- **Speak their Language:** Use language and jargon familiar to your customer. When your conversation mirrors their understanding, it can make the conversation more comfortable for them.
- **Show Genuine Thoughtfulness:** Lastly, express genuine concern and provide solutions to their problems. Showing that you genuinely care about their satisfaction can leave a lasting positive impression.

Mastering these integral techniques of understanding your customers and their needs forms the bedrock of any successful outbound sales strategy. A salesman who deeply understands their customers and empathetically communicates is a formidable force in the world of sales.

Chapter 9: Harnessing the Power of Cold Calling

Despite the rise of digital sales strategies, cold calling continues to play a vital role in outbound sales. Grasping this seemingly daunting task can have a game-changing impact on your sales performance. This chapter will delve into the art of cold calling and provide strategies to excel in this powerful sales technique.

Understanding the Purpose of Cold Calls

Before we dive into the specifics, it's essential to understand the fundamental goal of cold calling. In outbound sales, a cold call isn't meant to close a sale; instead, it's designed to open a dialogue, build rapport, and eventually forge a relationship. This bridge can later serve as a pathway to opportunities for making that critical sale.

Mastering the Art of the First Impressions

First impressions matter, especially in cold calls. Since it's a one-time chance to grasp the prospect's attention, your approach should be professional, confident, and friendly. A concise, clear, and captivating introduction is key. Before the call, take time to craft an introduction that concisely explains who you are, the reason for your call, and how the prospect stands to benefit from the conversation.

Research is Key

One of the common mistakes in cold calling is to dive in without any prior research on the prospect. Before you make a call, take a few minutes to learn about the prospect's company, their business model, challenges, and the industry they operate. Leverage tools like Linkedin, company websites, and industry reports to gather insights. This precall research will enhance your credibility and demonstrate that you're genuinely interested in helping the prospect, instead of just making a sale.

Personalization is Powerful

Nobody wants to feel like they are just another name on a list of cold calls. Always strive to keep the conversation personalized and relevant. Refer to the prospect by their name, align your product's benefits with their specific pain points, talk about their industry and, if possible, bring up a recent news about their company. This kind of personalization shows respect for their time and reveals your dedication.

Use Open-ended Questions

In outbound sales, a conversation is much more beneficial than a pitch. To navigate the conversation and keep it flowing, open-ended questions are your best tool. They encourage the prospect to speak about their business, goals, and challenges, giving you a deep understanding of their needs. More importantly, it makes the prospect feel heard and valued.

Overcoming Objections

In cold calling, rejections and objections are part and parcel of the process. But remember, an objection is just another opportunity to elucidate the value your product or service can provide. Be prepared with responses for common objections and always handle them with positivity and patience.

Following Up is Crucial

Even a fantastic cold call may not lead to an immediate outcome. This is where follow-ups come in. Persistence, with a balanced respect for the prospect's time and space, often pays off. You can follow-up via email, LinkedIn messages, or another call. But, ensure to deliver value in your follow ups, for example, by sharing helpful resources related to the prospect's industry or their challenges.

These strategies will not only enable you to excel in cold calling but also empower you to contribute positively to your prospects' success. Embrace the art of cold calling with an open mind, resilience, and zeal. Remember, it's not just about immediate sales, but building a relationship and value over time. It's this long-term vision that will truly elevate your outbound sales journey.

Section 4: Building and Managing a Successful Sales Team

4.1: Recruiting and Selecting the Right Sales Talent

Recruiting and selecting the right sales talent is an essential component in building and managing a successful sales team. One bad hire can slow team momentum and cause setbacks, whereas one star performer can massively boost team productivity and morale. This process begins with forming a clear understanding of what your ideal salesperson looks like.

Ideal Salesperson Profile

Before even thinking about getting the word out for your open sales roles, take the time to envision your ideal candidate. What kind of skills, qualifications, and character traits are you looking for? Keep in mind that while knowledge and experience are valuable, attributes like motivation, resilience, the ability to listen and learn quickly can sometimes prove to be more vital.

Marketing your Sales Position

To attract the right sales talent, it's equally important to market the position accurately. Clearly delineate the roles and responsibilities, key performance indicators, salary package, and company culture to help potential candidates assess whether they would be a good fit for your business. Furthermore, highlighting the growth opportunities offered by your company can be a great way to draw in ambitious candidates.

Screening and Interviewing Candidates

When screening resumes, look for indications of prior success in sales and consistency in employment. Candidates who exhibit willingness to work their way up and commit to a company for a reasonable period are usually good bets. In interviews, look beyond the candidate's ability to articulate well. Gauge their problem-solving abilities, listening skills, resilience, ability to handle rejection, and how well they can build rapport. Role-playing exercises can be useful in assessing such attributes.

Making the Hiring Decision

Check references diligently. Past behavior is usually a reliable indicator of future performance. When making the decision, consider their cultural fit with your company along with their qualifications and experience.

4.2: Training and Equipping your Sales Team

After you have got the right people on board, the next phase is to properly train and equip them. Irrespective of how experienced your salespeople are, they would need some training and input on your products and market.

Comprehensive Onboarding

Introduce your new hires to your company's mission, vision, culture, and internal systems. Outline their KPIs, sales targets, and performance incentives.

Ongoing Training

Sales techniques, market environments, and buyer habits change over time. Having a regular training program can help in updating your team's skills and knowledge, and reinforcing your sales process.

4.3: Leading and Motivating your Sales Team

A sales team's success doesn't just rely on the talent and skills of the team members, but equally on the quality of their leadership.

Creating a Positive Culture

A culture of respect, openness, encouragement, and healthy competition can foster motivation and performance. Recognize and reward success to reinforce desired behaviors.

Clear Communication

Set clear expectations, provide regular feedback, and be transparent about the company's objectives and performance. Support your team by addressing any obstacles they face.

4.4: Monitoring and Evaluating Performance

Implement systems for tracking and analyzing your team's performance.

Key Performance Indicators

Establish clear KPIs to measure both individual and team performance. KPIs can include sales volume, revenue, conversion rates, and average deal size.

Regular Reviews

Conduct regular performance reviews. This will aid in identifying issues early on and addressing them through coaching or additional training.

Using CRM Systems

CRM systems can provide valuable data for assessing performance, streamlining your sales process, and forecasting sales.

The process of building and managing a successful sales team is, in essence, a cycle of recruitment, training, motivating, evaluating, and back to recruitment. Each phase is an equally critical part of the 'engine' that powers your sales team towards success.

Subsection 4.1: Assembling an Outstanding Sales Team

Building a successful outbound sales team begins with hiring the right people. Inbound tactics won't be effective without a competent team to execute them. Frame your search around individuals who are not just skilled, but also have the right attitude and leverage it towards achieving your business objectives.

4.1.1: Begin with the Hiring Process

Rigorous selection helps in ascertaining that the team members are fairly treated during the hiring process. Regardless of if you're employing former acquaintances or first-time job seekers, the criteria should remain consistent. This assures you that you're not leaving any stones unturned during your search for quality sales representatives.

4.1.2: Ingrain Your Business Philosophy in Your Team

You should ensure your team understands and internalizes the company's philosophy to streamline their operations. This cohesion is vital for accomplishing team goals. Your sales team should, for instance, be clear on the product or service they're selling, who your primary customers are, and what makes the company unique from its competitors.

4.1.3: Train Your Employees

Providing regular training sessions to your sales team has massive, long-term benefits. Routine training doesn't just help to integrate new sales tactics and strategies into the team, but makes your sales staff feel more valuable and appreciated, improving morale and job satisfaction.

4.1.4: Set Clear and Attainable Sales Goals

You should set clear, achievable goals for your team members. Understanding what's expected creates a work environment that fosters proficiency and efficiency. Also, when employees meet the set goals, they feel accomplished and motivated.

4.1.5: Cultivate a Positive Sales Culture

Cultivating a positive sales culture will directly increase your sales team's performance. The culture should inspire the employees to do their best, interact professionally, respect each other and contribute to team success. Team building activities outside of work can also foster a strong relationship between team members and improve productivity.

4.1.6: Monitor and Evaluate Performance

Performance monitoring is essential for identifying areas that need improvement. It gives you a chance to reward top performers and motivate low performers to improve. Using measurable metrics will help you evaluate your team fairly and accurately.

4.1.7: Provide Constructive Feedback

Finally, providing constructive feedback helps your team know how they are performing and gives them a clear path to improvement. This should always be communicated promptly, and in a manner that encourages and motivates them.

Conclusion

Remember, since your sales team literally owns the revenue-generating function of your company, the importance of assembling, nurturing and managing an excellent sales team cannot be emphasized enough. It requires patience, knowledge, and understanding. But with consistent effort, you can indeed build a world-class team that will transform your business significantly.

4.1 Cultivating a High-Performing Sales Environment

A successful sales team doesn't just magically happen. It is the result of a purposeful and strategic effort by sales leaders to create an environment that cultivates high performance. In order to achieve this, leaders must understand every member of their team, including their strengths, weaknesses, and what motivates them.

Understanding Each Team Member

The first key to building a successful sales team is understanding each team member. This process starts during the hiring phase with thorough interviews and appropriate vetting tools like personality assessments. But it doesn't stop there. Even after a salesperson is onboarded, continuous one-on-one's, coaching and performance reviews are essential to gauge their progress and potential.

Remember that every salesperson is unique - they possess different skills, experience levels and work ethics. As their manager, it is your responsibility to discern their capabilities and place them in a role where they can flourish. While doing this, also focus on their areas of improvements and provide them with necessary training and coaching.

Setting Clear Expectations

Communicating expectations helps salespeople understand their roles better. Leadership should set clear, measurable goals for the team and each individual. Goals should be realistic but challenging, driving each salesperson to constantly improve.

Encouraging Teamwork and Collaboration

"Sales" might often be associated with competition, but the reality is that the best sales teams operate on collaboration and teamwork. Instigate a culture where team members share ideas, insights and strategies. Organizing team-building activities can foster camaraderie among team members. Moreover, acknowledging and rewarding collaborative behavior will further encourage the team to work together.

Foster Growth Mindset

A growth mindset is key to outbound sales mastery. Encourage your team members to regard challenges as opportunities to grow. Make sure they understand that failing isn't necessarily a bad thing, but rather an opening for learning and development. Support them in enhancing their skills and knowledge through constant feedback, training and encouragement.

Implementing a Robust Reward and Recognition System

A successful sales team is highly motivated. One effective way of promoting motivation is through a robust reward and recognition system. Commissions are standard in the sales industry, but think beyond money. Recognize hard work and dedication, celebrate wins and milestones, and give credit where credit is due.

Leveraging Technology

In today's digital age, incorporating technology is inevitable if you want your sales team to thrive. Customer Relationship Management (CRM) systems, sales analytics, automations, and AI-powered tools can optimize your sales operations, making your team more productive and efficient.

Continuous Learning and Development

Outbound sales mastery is a journey, not a destination. The most successful sales teams continue to learn, adapt, and grow. Foster a culture of continuous learning and professional development, whether it's through continuous training, workshops, or exposure to industry events.

At the end of the day, the success of your sales team hinges on how well they are led and managed. As a sales leader, you must continuously mold and shape your team, helping them to develop their skills, boost their confidence, and maximize their potential. If you can do this, you'll cultivate a high-performing sales environment that can transform both lives and businesses.

Building and managing a successful sales team can be a daunting task, but with solid strategies, dedication, and a clear vision, you can create an unbeatable team that will drive your organization to greater heights.

Subsection 4.1: Cultivating a Winning Sales Culture

The foundation of a successful sales team is a robust and empowering sales culture. It's essential to foster a positive and high-energy environment that encourages team members to strive for exceeding targets and making a significant contribution to the organization's objectives.

Creating a Vision

Cultivating a winning sales culture starts with creating a compelling vision for your team. Your vision should articulate what you are aiming to achieve and why it's essential. Moreover, it should be inspiring enough to motivate your team members to bring their best to the table every day.

Setting Clear Goals and Objectives

Once you establish a powerful vision, it's crucial to set clear goals and objectives. Each team member should know what is expected from them and how their performance will be measured. The goals should be SMART – Specific, Measurable, Achievable, Relevant, and Time-bound.

Recognizing and Rewarding Performance

Another significant aspect of a productive sales culture is recognition and reward. Celebrate the wins, big or small, and make it a point to acknowledge the efforts of your team members. Recognizing achievements and efforts is a powerful motivator and can significantly boost morale and productivity.

Encouraging Continuous Learning

Outbound sales mastery requires constant learning and adaptation. Encourage your team members to learn new strategies, techniques, and tools to enhance their performance. Regular training and development sessions, workshops, seminars, and team-building exercises can help in skill development.

Communication is Key

Transparent, open, and regular communication can immensely support a positive sales culture. Address concerns, provide feedback, and keep your team updated about any changes or developments.

Teamwork and Collaboration

Promote a sense of unity and cooperation within your team. Encourage mutual assistance and knowledge sharing. This will not only boost team performance but also cultivate a sense of belonging among team members.

Subsection 4.2: Recruiting and Retaining Top Talent

A successful sales team is made up of talented, motivated, and competent individuals.

Attracting Talent

You can attract top talent by advertising a position's benefits and opportunities for growth. Describe the team culture, work-life balance, and other perks that can attract potential candidates.

Hiring Process

During the hiring process, look for candidates who not only have the right sales skills but also align with your organization's culture and values. Use competency-based interviews and assessments to evaluate their skills and capabilities.

Onboarding Process

A smooth onboarding process can significantly increase new hire's productivity. Ensure new team members understand their roles and responsibilities, the team's goals, work dynamics, and overall sales process.

Retention

Retaining top talent can be a significant challenge. To encourage retention, ensure your team members feel valued, recognized, and rewarded for their efforts. Provide growth opportunities, continuous learning and development initiatives, and maintain a happy work-life balance.

Subsection 4.3: Strategic Sales Planning

Strategic sales planning involves setting targets, customer segmentation, identifying potential markets, and planning the tactics to reach those goals.

Developing a Sales Plan

A sales plan outlines the specific strategies and tactics your team will implement to hit the sales targets. The sales plan should align with your organization's broader strategic plan.

Implementing the Plan

The implementation phase, involves communicating the plan to your team, assigning roles, and constantly reviewing and adjusting the plan as needed. Regular team meetings can help to keep everyone focused and on track.

Subsection 4.4: Monitoring and Optimization of Sales Performance

A great sales leader keeps a close eye on their team's performance and continually looks for ways to improve.

Performance Analytics

Use CRM tools and other analytics software to monitor sales performance. Check the pipeline progress, track quota attainment, and look at other relevant sales metrics.

Regular Feedback

Provide regular feedback to your team members. Celebrate accomplishments, provide constructive feedback, and discuss areas for improvement.

Sales Coaching

Sales coaching can significantly improve your team's performance. Identify areas where team members are struggling and provide one-on-one coaching to address those issues. Encourage team members to learn from each other and share best practices.

Harnessing outbound sales mastery is a continuous journey. Constantly learning, adapting to changes, and striving to improve are keys to building and managing a successful sales team. Set high standards, inspire your team to reach those standards, and create an environment conducive to success.

Subsection 4.1: Principles of Effective Sales Team Management

To attain mastery in outbound sales, establishing an adroit sales team is imperative. Before you learn how to manage a successful sales team, you need to understand the principles of effective sales team management. Mastering these principles will help you navigate through various challenges that may arise in the sales process and will enable your team to reach their potential.

4.1.1 Setting Clear Objectives

Clearly outline the sales goals that your team has to accomplish. These could be daily, weekly, monthly, or annual targets. High clarity on targets will not only help your team members align their efforts but also allow them to visualize their progress. Make sure these goals are SMART - Specific, Measurable, Achievable, Relevant, and Time-bound.

4.1.2 Building a Collaborative Environment

Each team member brings a unique set of skills and experiences. A collaborative environment helps in nurturing these skills, facilitating learning, and promoting collective problem-solving. Utilize different communication and collaboration tools to foster this environment.

4.1.3 Regular Training and Development

The outbound sales landscape is constantly evolving - new technologies, changing customer expectations, and an increasingly competitive environment. By regularly training your team on new sales techniques, tools, and market trends, you enable them to stay ahead of the curve.

4.1.4 Leveraging Sales Technology

Investing in sales tools and technology facilitates automation of repetitive tasks, reduces errors, and enhances productivity. It saves time and effort that can then be directed towards strategizing and nurturing customer relationships.

4.1.5 Providing Constructive Feedback

Feedback is crucial for improvement. Ensure that your team frequently receives constructive feedback to identify areas of improvement. Celebrate their victories, however small, and guide them patiently through their mistakes.

4.1.6 Monitoring and Adjusting Sales Strategies

Outbound sales strategies need to be revisited and adjusted based on real-time performances. Utilizing sales metrics and analytics, identify sales patterns and behaviors. This will help you tweak your strategy to meet your sales objectives.

4.1.7 Building a Culture of Trust and Respect

While performance is important, so is morality. A culture of trust and respect nurtures positivity and motivates team members to give their best. Encourage open discussions and make your team feel heard and valued.

In the subsequent sections, you will learn how to apply these principles for specific aspects of sales team management, such as hiring the right talent, developing a strong sales culture, leveraging sales technology, and conducting regular sales training. By doing so, you'll be able to transform your sales team into a well-oiled machine, thereby leading to a substantial increase in outbound sales performance and inevitably, transforming lives and businesses.

Section 5: Harnessing the Power of Digital Tools in Sales

Subsection 5.1: Embracing Customer Relationship Management (CRM) Systems in Outbound Sales

As outbound sales evolve, digital tools are increasingly becoming central to mastering the processes and gaining a competitive edge. The tools not only streamline sales operations but also transform the outcomes. One of the key digital tools is the Customer Relationship Management (CRM) system, an integral technological component in today's sales arena.

Understanding CRM Systems

A CRM system is essentially a type of software designed to manage your company's interactions with current and potential customers. By using data analysis about a customer's history with your company, it can enhance business relationships with customers, focusing on customer retention and driving sales growth. Few CRM systems even offer automation of repetitive tasks, allowing sales reps to focus on more critical aspects of the sales process.

Key Elements of CRM Systems

CRM systems are equipped with several vital elements that facilitate efficient outbound sales.

- **Contact Management:** CRM systems store essential details about prospects and customers, such as contact details, interaction history, and transaction records. The easy accessibility to such vital information significantly simplifies lead prioritization and follow-up processes.
- **Task Management:** It helps salespeople track vital sales tasks, deadlines, and progress, ensuring they don't miss out on any crucial milestones or follow-ups in the sales cycle.
- **Reporting and Analytics:** CRM systems offer data-driven insights about sales performance, customer behavior, and market trends. These insights aid in formulating effective outbound sales strategies and decisions.
- **Social Media Integration:** Many CRM systems come with an integrated feature that connects to social media platforms, giving sales reps a comprehensive view of their prospect's online behavior and interests.
- **Sales Automation:** CRM tools can automate administrative tasks that often consume unnecessary

time, enabling salespeople to spend more time on revenue-generating tasks.

How CRM Benefits Outbound Sales

CRM's benefits in outbound sales cannot be overstated. It offers several advantages that can truly transform an organization's sales process.

- **Improved Customer Relations:** CRM systems facilitate personalized interactions by providing detailed customer history and preferences. This personalized communication can significantly enhance customer experience and satisfaction.
- **Increased Sales Productivity:** The automation of administrative tasks and easy access to vital customer information save time for sales reps, leading to increased sales productivity.
- **Better Decision Making:** The data-driven insights provided by CRM systems aid in making informed sales decisions, thus reducing risks and increasing chances of success.
- **Enhanced Team Collaboration:** Shared customer data and task management features improve collaboration among sales team members, leading to better results.
- **Higher Revenues:** CRM systems enable sales teams to pursue the right leads and opportunities, thus leading to more conversions and higher revenues.

In conclusion, the life of a salesperson can be made significantly easier by harnessing the power of CRM systems. A well-utilized CRM system not only boosts sale productivity but also improves customer satisfaction, paving the way for a durable relationship. Successfully implementing CRM systems in your outbound sales strategy is not an option but an essential move in today's digital age.

Subsection 5.1: Efficient Use of Customer Relationship Management (CRM) Systems in Outbound Sales Strategy

In the modern sales landscape where personalization and Relationship Marketing are at the center stage, Customer Relationship Management (CRM) tools have morphed into an essential part of every successful business strategy. These digital tools help businesses track, manage, and analyse all their customer interactions and data, ensuring these interactions are as effective as possible.

Understanding CRM

A CRM system is software that centralizes, simplifies, secures and scales customer engagement. From managing contact information and sales opportunities, to continuous follow-up and reporting, it integrates all these touchpoints into a single, yet cohesive customer view, thereby providing crucial help in fostering long-term customer relationships.

CRM-tools are not strictly about sales, but about putting your customers first—monumentally modifying the prognosis of sells in the process. Essentially, CRM pivots around a concept that is inextricably connected to the outbound sales effort: creating value for the customer and increasing their overall satisfaction. This, in turn, boosts sales, profitability and customer retention.

Leveraging CRM for Sales Outcomes

Digital transformation and CRM tools have had a dramatic impact on outbound sales strategies, causing a shift to smarter, organized, efficient and effective processes that can manage complex deals and long sales cycles. Here's how these systems play an integral role:

- **Information Management:** CRM systems enable businesses to bring together, in one place, all data associated with customers. Customer profiles include contact information, interaction history, social media activity, and often even information about customer behaviour and habits, enabling sales reps to deliver personalized experiences.
- **Sales Force Automation (SFA):** CRM software automates sales tasks such as order processing, contact management, information sharing, order tracking, inventory monitoring, sales forecasting, and performance evaluation. This reduces manual labor adding efficiency into the process.
- **Pipeline Management:** CRM software allows tracking of the sales pipeline. Sales reps can manage stages of the sales process for each potential sale, identify bottlenecks, and understand the sales funnel better. This leads to optimized conversions and forecasting.
- **Communication:** CRM system can help businesses improve their communication with customers and prospects as the reps can effortlessly select and segregate customers according to specified criteria and can hence interact with them accordingly. They can also track the history of communication to serve customers better.

Selecting a CRM Tool

When selecting a CRM tool, it is crucial to consider the needs, size, targets, and industry of your business. Some popular CRM systems widely used today include Salesforce, Microsoft Dynamics, HubSpot, and Zoho CRM.

The power of the CRM tool is scalable, i.e., it possesses the ability to grow with your organization, ensuring longevity and cost-effectiveness. When properly implemented, a good CRM system will offer you a clear overview of your customers. You can see everything from preferred products/services to any outstanding customer service issues and can react accordingly.

As an outbound sales strategist, transforming your business through digital tools like CRM, it's all about understanding your customers—making sense of their needs, and responding effectively and efficiently. The digital realm has put customers in control of the purchasing process. Harnessing tools like CRM, allows businesses to meet clients where they are, setting you apart in a crowded marketplace.

With the proper implementation and efficient use of CRM, you can maximize your outbound sales, improve customer satisfaction, thereby marking a step further in mastering outbound sales. Remember, it's not just about closing the next deal—it's ultimately about building a potential long-term partnership with your customers.

5.1 Leveraging CRM for Enhanced Sales Performance

One of the most crucial elements in today's digital sales environments is Customer Relationship Management (CRM). CRM systems form the core of diligent information handling, targeted customer engagement, and strategic decision-making.

Understanding CRM and its Advantages

A CRM software helps a company manage relationships and interactions with prospective, current, and previous customers. It's a transformative digital tool for outbound sales, designed to enhance profitability while ensuring customer satisfaction.

Here are the primary benefits of using a CRM system in your sales efforts:

1. Organized Information

CRM systems provide an organized, comprehensive view of customer details and history. The software gathers and sorts essential data such as customer contacts, purchase histories, preferences, and even feedback. This accessibility of information helps salespeople understand the client better, leading to more personalized sales tactics.

2. Streamlined Communication

Instead of drowning in a sea of emails, calls, notes, and meetings, salespeople can streamline their communication via the CRM system. The software logs every interaction with the customer, ensuring no important information gets lost and allows each team member to stay updated about customer interactions.

3. Enhanced Customer Service

Quickly resolving questions and complaints is crucial for maintaining customer satisfaction. With a CRM system, every question, discussion, purchase, or service request gets documented. This knowledge empowers the sales team, enabling them to provide prompt and accurate responses to customer queries and complaints.

4. Efficiency and Productivity

By automating routine tasks, CRM frees up salespeople's time, enabling them to focus more on selling. The platform can hail qualified leads, schedule follow-ups, and send reminders, making the sales process more manageable.

5. Related Analytics

Functionally rich CRM systems come with analytics that can help salespeople make data-driven decisions. Through detailed insights and forecasting, sales teams can better understand and adapt their sales strategies.

Selecting the appropriate CRM

The choice of CRM depends heavily on a business's unique requirements, objectives, and budget. However, a versatile CRM solution should at least have the following:

1. Ease of use

The system should be user-friendly, with a clean interface and intuitive navigation.

2. Flexibility

The CRM should be customizable, to align seamlessly with your company's workflow and processes.

3. Mobile accessibility

It should offer mobile access, allowing the sales team to operate from anywhere at any time.

4. Integration capabilities

The CRM should easily integrate with other existing software, like email services, social media platforms, or analytics tools.

5. Reliable customer support

A good CRM solution will have reliable customer support to address any technical issues or inquiries promptly and efficiently.

In the digital age, deploying a CRM system is no longer a luxury but a necessity for any outbound sales team. These systems facilitate better communication, improve operational efficiency, and help sales teams build stronger relationships with their customers. However, remember to choose a CRM that aligns best with your business model and goals, as well as train your team for its efficient use. In the end, a tool only proves effective when used correctly.

Subsection 5.1: Utilizing Customer Relationship Management (CRM) Systems for Optimizing Outbound Sales

In a modern sales environment, digital tools aren't just a fancy addition; they are crucial to your success. One of the key digital tools in outbound sales is a Customer Relationship Management (CRM) system. This powerful platform is the backbone of your sales process, offering unparalleled benefits in customer tracking, relationship management, and sales optimization.

What is a CRM System?

A CRM system is more than just a fancy address book. At its core, the CRM is designed to help you manage all your customer data, interactions, and other essential sales activities. It is a sophisticated digital tool that enables you to keep track of leads, prospects, existing customers, and all data associated with them. This includes customer backgrounds, contact information, past interactions, and so forth.

Why Use a CRM in Outbound Sales?

One might think that having a physical record of customer data is good enough. However, there are various reasons why abandoning the old methods for a CRM system can revolutionize your outbound sales efforts.

Accessibility and Organization

CRM systems allow easy accessibility and organization of customer data, which can give your team a competitive edge. Being able to search and find customer information quickly can significantly enhance productivity, thus reducing sales cycles and, ultimately, increasing revenue.

Effective Communication

CRM systems enable effective communication. For example, instead of carrying a physical binder with leads' information or saving them to spreadsheets, CRM systems allow for greater flexibility. All details about a lead or opportunities are kept updated in real time, ensuring everyone in the team is on the same page, fostering collaboration and efficiency.

Better Tracking

CRM systems offer stellar tracking capabilities, allowing you to follow the buyer's journey from prospect to customer. From tracking the number of interactions, to understanding conversion rates, CRM tools ease the process of keeping an eye on key performance indicators (KPIs). That way, you can assess the effectiveness of your sales strategy in real time, and make changes as necessary.

Enhanced Customer Relationship Management

CRM systems allow you to personalize your outreach strategy, which can significantly improve customer experience. With detailed records of past interactions, preferences, and pain points, sales reps can tailor their approach accordingly. This can lead to increased customer satisfaction, higher sales, and more repeat business.

CRM Systems and Future Trends

As we move further into the digital age, CRM systems will continue to evolve and become more interconnected with other digital tools. For example, integrating CRM with email marketing software to facilitate automated emails, or with predictive analytics software to forecast sales trends. Those who get on board early and learn to utilize these tools effectively will have a significant advantage in their outbound sales efforts.

Key Takeaways

In conclusion, integrating a CRM system into your outbound sales process is not just about staying up-to-date with the latest technology. It's about optimizing your sales process, improving your team's productivity, and revolutionizing your customer approach. Remember, the goal of any good sales process is to put the customer first - and with CRM systems, this becomes an achievable target.

In the next subsection, we'll talk about 'Leveraging Social Media Platforms for Outbound Sales'. This will involve understanding the varied functionalities and potential of various social media platforms in unearthing fruitful leads.

Chapter 5.1: Leveraging Customer Relationship Management (CRM) Tools

In the rapidly evolving digital landscape, mastering sales is no longer limited to being a smooth talker or having a knack for persuasion. Today, successful salespeople also necessarily need command over digital tools – particularly Customer Relationship Management (CRM) tools, which can empower them in the entire sales process. In this chapter, we will unpack how CRM tools provide an edge in outbound sales and why they're essential for sales mastery.

5.1.1: Understanding CRM

CRM tools are software systems developed to manage all your company's relationships and interactions with potential and current customers. They can be a storehouse of crucial information about your customers, including their contact details, communication history, preferences, past purchases, and more. This knowledge can provide you with a comprehensive overview of your customers, enabling you to nurture relationships, identify sales opportunities, streamline processes, and improve profitability.

5.1.2: Scalable Outreach with CRM

As your leads increase, you need a system that digitally oversees and organizes all customer interactions in one place. CRM software allows salespeople to manage thousands of contacts without compromising the personalized approach to each lead. A CRM enables you to segment leads based on various factors such as their prospect status, location, industry, and even preferences. This helps in designing personalized outreach strategies that tend to have a higher success rate.

5.1.3 Automating Tasks with CRM

Manual data entry, follow-up reminders, scheduling meetings, recording communications, updating statuses – these seemingly mundane tasks can consume a considerable amount of a salesperson's day. CRM tools come equipped with features that can automate these tasks, leaving you with more time to interact with customers.

5.1.4: CRM as a Treasure Trove of Analytics

CRM tools automatically gather data from numerous touchpoints throughout the customer journey, storing it ready for use. This data is a treasure trove that can shed light on customer behaviors, market trends, sales performance, and more. Through CRM analytics, you can unearth insights like when it's best to contact a customer, which marketing techniques work best for different segments, or which products or services are performing well.

5.1.5: Exceeding Customer Expectations with CRM

With updates on real-time customer interactions, CRM ensures that you are never out of the loop about what's happening with your customers. This knowledge aids in delivering prompt and relevant responses to customers' queries and complaints, thereby elevating customer experience. Besides, by engaging customers right when they're ready, you can seize sales opportunities and increase conversions.

5.1.6: Collaboration in Teams Through CRM

Sales are seldom a one-person show. Successful closing often involves coordinated efforts of different teams - sales, marketing, technical, customer service, etc. By providing access to customer data on a unified platform, CRM systems enhance interdepartmental collaboration, aligning everyone towards the common objective of winning over the customer.

As the world of sales continues to expand into the digital realm, mastering tools like a CRM system can give you an unmatched advantage. It is an investment that can facilitate optimized customer interactions, keep you informed, save time, and streamline efforts. In the next chapters, we will delve deeper into other digital tools that promise to revolutionize the way outbound sales functions!

Section 6: Effective Communication and Negotiation Skills

Subsection 6.1: Understanding the Power of Active Listening

When we talk about communication, we often think about it in terms of articulating our thoughts, ideas, persuasions, propositions, and selling skills. However, one half of the communication process that is often overlooked and undervalued is that of listening—active listening to be precise. In the realm of outbound sales, an understanding and mastery of active listening skills can enhance your ability to comprehend your prospects' needs, build trust, and foster long-lasting relationships that not just culminate in a successful sale, but open avenues for future business as well.

Why is Active Listening Important?

In the heat of making a sale, the temptation to dominate the conversation can often be overwhelming. After all, the more convincingly you speak about the product or service you are selling, the better chances you have of making a sale, right? Not quite. The reality is that sales conversations should always be two-way streets. Your prospects want to feel heard, understood, and valued, and that's where active listening comes in.

Active listening entails not only hearing the words that another person is saying but, even more importantly, understanding and interpreting the complete message being sent. When you actively listen, you empathize with your prospects, validate their concerns, seek clarity, and refrain from planning your response or rebuttal. Consequently, you create a secure conversational space that enables honest exchanges and effective negotiations.

The Role of Active Listening in Negotiation

Now, let's delve further into how active listening plays a direct role in negotiation. Every sale involves some degree of negotiation — can you offer a better price? Is your product's quality superior? Can your services be delivered faster? Such are the questions that customers might have.

Negotiation can be a make or break point in a sale. Remember that discord is common in negotiations, and it's often not about who speaks the loudest, but who listens the most. Through active listening, you invite openness. You get to gain insight into what the customer really needs or what problem they're trying to solve. Deep understanding breeds empathy—and empathy has a magical way of softening hard-line stances. When your clients feel understood, they are more likely to compromise, leading to mutually beneficial agreements.

How to Improve Your Active Listening Skills

Active listening is not a trait we are born with; it's a skill. And as a skill, it can be developed and improved. Here are some techniques you can use:

- **Give your complete attention**: We are often subtly or unconsciously preoccupied— planning the next pitch, thinking about a previous call, or maybe distracted by the environment. Let go of these distractions. Be present in the conversation completely, both mentally and physically.
- **Validate feelings and concerns**: Show your prospects that you recognize their feelings. You could say, "I understand that you're concerned about….". Validation encourages more open dialogue.

- **Ask thought-provoking questions**: Instead of responding directly to a client's concern, try to delve deeper by asking questions. For instance, if a client mentions that they find your product expensive, rather than justifying the price right away, you could ask, "Could you elaborate more on what features you feel don't justify the cost?". This way, you get a better understanding of your client's value perception.
- **Check for understanding**: Reiterate, paraphrase, or summarize the main points of your prospect's message to ensure you've understood correctly. This not only keeps miscommunications at bay but also communicates to your prospects that you've been listening attentively.

The art of communication is laden with subtleties. In the quest to conquer the sales world, always remember what Stephen R. Covey, a renowned self-help author, once said, "Most people do not listen with the intent to understand; they listen with the intent to reply." Break the conventional mold, and practice active listening to discover a transformative influence on your outbound sales endeavors.

Chapter 6.1: The Art of Active Listening: Mastering Communications in Outbound Sales

One of the key components of successful outbound sales is active listening. Being an active listener means fully concentrating on, understanding, responding and then remembering what is being said. It means prioritizing your customer's needs, desires and concerns over the script you have prepared.

Understanding Active Listening

To master active listening, it is crucial to first understand what it means. Active listening is not merely about hearing words; it involves decoding the message encoded in words. It's about picking up verbal and non-verbal cues to understand the speaker's (in this case, the customer's) emotions, needs, and concerns.

Role of Active Listening in Sales

Active listening forms the foundation of effective communication in sales. It is through active listening that you can create personalized solutions for your customers, build relationships, and close sales more effectively. It allows you to:

1. Understand customers' needs
2. Recognize their buying signals
3. Address their objections
4. Provide personalized solutions
5. Build trust and rapport

Techniques for Active Listening

Following are some practical techniques you can use to improve your active listening skills:

1. Give Full Attention

Ensure you're not multi-tasking or distracted when you're talking to a customer. Show them they have your complete attention, and they are valuable to you.

2. Non-Verbal Communication

Non-verbal cues are crucial in communicating your attentiveness. Making eye contact, nodding your head in understanding, and mirroring their emotions can help you establish a connection.

3. Ask Open-Ended Questions

Open-ended questions can help you delve deeper into customer's needs, beliefs, and concerns. They give your customer an opportunity to speak, helping you understand them better.

4. Use Paraphrasing

Paraphrasing or summarizing their needs and stating them back assures your customer that they've been understood correctly.

5. Encourage Conversation

Encourage customers to express their thoughts and feelings. Avoid interrupting them and give them enough time to finish conveying their message.

Challenges to Active Listening

Active listening, though crucial, isn't always easy. Often, obstacles appear in the form of:

- Preoccupation with your own thoughts
- Judgmental attitude
- Interrupting the speaker

- Lack of focus
- Physical and emotional disturbances

Recognizing and addressing these challenges is crucial to improving your active listening skills.

Sharpening Your Skills

Active listening is not a natural gift; it's a skill that can be honed over time. Regular self-evaluation, seeking feedback, role-playing, and practicing mindfulness can help.

In summary, mastering active listening is an integral factor in achieving outbound sales mastery. With earnest efforts, continual practice, and the genuine intent to understand customers, you can turn active listening into a powerhouse skill that transforms lives and businesses alike.

Subsection 6.1: The Power of Active Listening in Sales

In the realm of outbound sales, one critical communication skill that often gets overlooked is active listening. Active listening is where a sales representative genuinely listens to the perspective of a potential customer, comprehends their needs, and responds accordingly. A mastery of this skill enhances your ability to communicate effectively and negotiate efficiently with prospects, offering multiple benefits such as building a rapport, understanding customers' needs, and fostering strong customer relationships.

Understanding the Art of Active Listening

Contrary to common belief, listening is more than just hearing. While hearing is a passive process, active listening is a conscious act of paying full attention to the speaker, absorbing, understanding the information conveyed, and responding thoughtfully. Active listening involves three main components:

1. Comprehension: This is the basic level of listening that most sales representatives engage in. Comprehension requires understanding the words and phrases that the customer uses, along with their specific meaning related to the context.
2. Retention: Retention involves storing and recalling information in your memory. This can be useful when you want to reference a detail from earlier in the conversation as it shows the customer that you're genuinely attentive to their needs.
3. Response: The practical demonstration of understanding. Once you have comprehended and retained the information provided by the customer, the next step is to offer a relevant and precise response that caters to the customer's needs.

Building Rapport through Active Listening

Active listening can play a significant role in relationship building. Customers appreciate when sales representatives give them the freedom to express their concerns and when they feel heard. Empathy plays a crucial role here. By expressing understanding and validating the customer's feelings, you also build trust, making it easier for you to navigate the sales conversation and steer it towards a positive outcome.

Understanding Customer's Needs through Active Listening

In outbound sales, the success in converting a prospect to a customer highly depends on how well you understand their needs and offer them a personalized solution. Active listening provides you with a window into those needs. Probing questions and paraphrasing the customer's comments can help confirm understanding and make the customer feel appreciated.

Strengthening Negotiation Skills via Active Listening

Active listening plays a pivotal role in the negotiation process by helping you decipher the needs, reservations, and motivations of your prospect. By creating a dialogue that encourages prospects to express themselves openly, you'll be able to understand their viewpoint, counter objections effectively, and cleverly position your product or service as the solution to their problems.

How to Develop and Improve Active Listening Skills

Improving active listening skills requires regular practice and constant engagement in mindful conversations. Here are a few strategies:

- Be fully in the moment, focusing completely on the speaker.
- Avoid distractions such as phones or laptops during conversations.
- Use verbal and non-verbal gestures such as nodding, maintaining eye contact, and using affirmative phrases.
- Regularly provide feedback, ask open-ended questions, or rephrase points for clarity.

In conclusion, active listening is a potent tool that can improve your communication and negotiation skills in outbound sales. By mastering it, you not only empower yourself to better understand your prospective customers but also position yourself as a trusted advisor, making the sales journey rewarding for you and the customer alike.

Subsection 6.1: Understanding the Power of Listening

As you navigate the world of outbound sales, understanding the power of listening is crucial. Many sales professionals tend to believe that making a sale is about speaking — laying out the value proposition, delivering a compelling pitch, wrapping up with a strong call to action. But in truth, effective outbound sales work on a 2:1 ratio – listen twice as much as you talk.

Listening, in this context, goes beyond just hearing what the prospect is saying. It involves "active listening," which requires complete focus and understanding of verbal and non-verbal cues. Actively involving in a conversation enables you to catch the nuances, concerns, and underlying meanings that can help shape your sales pitch.

Subsection 6.2: Clear and Concise Communication

Being able to effectively express yourself is another pillar of outbound sales. This doesn't mean using complex industry jargon or wowing with lengthy speeches. On the contrary, your prospects will appreciate clear, concise, and easy-to-understand language that directly speaks to their pain points.

The key here is to simplify your product's value and how it can solve the clients' issues. Make your prospects see that you are on their side and that your goal is to help them address their problems effectively using your solution.

Subsection 6.3: Reading Non-Verbal Cues

Often, what isn't said in a conversation carries as much weight as the words spoken. Non-verbal cues are a major part of effective communication. These could be the prospect's body language, tone of voice, or even slight changes in their demeanor.

By reading these non-verbal signals, you can gauge the prospect's interest level, know the best time to interject your input, and when you might need to change your approach. It's a skill that requires practice but can strongly enhance your sales proficiency when correctly implemented.

Subsection 6.4: The Art of Persuasion

Mastering the art of persuasion is key in outbound sales. You need to convince prospects to share their pain points with you, trust your solutions, and finally, make a purchase. To be persuasive, you need a blend of confidence, understanding, empathy, and effective communication.

The goal is not to manipulate but rather to build meaningful relationships with your prospects based on trust and mutual benefit. Your genuine intent to help will surely shine through in your conversations and significantly contribute to your persuasiveness.

Subsection 6.5: Negotiation Skills

For every outbound sales professional, negotiation can be either a deal maker or a deal-breaker. It heavily relies on effective communication and deep understanding, but it's a standalone art and science by itself.

The essence of negotiation is to find mutual ground where both you and the prospect find value. Understanding of the prospect's needs, your own sales objectives, and the constraints will guide your negotiation strategy.

In a nutshell, effective communication and negotiation skills are vital for outbound sales mastery. By honing these skills, you'll be well-prepared to succeed in the ever-changing landscape of outbound sales.

Subsection 6.1: Understanding the Role of Clarity in Communication

The simplest but most crucial aspect of your outbound sales mastery is clear and concise communication. Remember, one of the goals of your sales pitch is to successfully and quickly convey your ideas or offerings to the potential customer, and the key to this success is a crystal clear articulation of thoughts. In the absence of clear communication, the misunderstanding can give rise to conflicts, failed tasks, and even lost sales.

To put it in perspective, let's understand a common scenario. Suppose you've reached out to a potential customer with your product that you believe can solve their problem, but somehow, the recipient is unable to understand its features, benefits, or its exact use. Despite having an excellent product or service, the deal may never close due to poorly communicated information.

Therefore, it's essential to prioritize clarity while communicating your offerings. Here are some practical tips that you can incorporate:

1. Understand Your Offering: Before you even begin to explain it to your lead, ensure that you thoroughly understand what you're selling. Understand the product or service inside and out, its features, advantages, potential use-cases, competitive edge etc. When you understand your product, it becomes easier to explain it to others.

2. Avoid Jargon: Wherever possible, avoid using industry-specific jargon when explaining your product or service to customers. Not everyone may be familiar with the terms, acronyms, or abbreviations you use every day in your industry. Presenting your offering in easily understandable language improves the chances of the prospect understanding and engaging with your product.

3. Use Examples and Stories: Sharing relatable examples or success stories can be incredibly effective, not just to illustrate how your product or service works, but also to generate enthusiasm and interest around it.

4. Confirm Understanding: After explaining the product or idea, check with the potential client to make sure they have understood correctly. Ask them to summarize their understanding or ask questions. This gives you a chance to rectify any misinterpretation or confusion right on the spot, ensuring that the lead fully grasps what you are offering.

Subsection 6.2: Harnessing The Power of Active Listening

Active listening is a crucial skill for effective communication, especially in sales. It involves fully focusing on the speaker, refraining from interruptions, and responding thoughtfully to what is being said. This makes the speaker feel heard and understood, creating a positive impact and nurturing trust in your relationship – a critical factor in closing sales.

Some active listening techniques include paraphrasing to show understanding, asking open-ended questions to encourage detail, and using verbal affirmations (like "uh-huh", "I see") to show engagement. By using active listening, you can understand the potential customer's needs, preferences, and challenges better, enabling you to pitch your product or service more effectively.

Subsection 6.3: Mastering the Art of Persuasion

Persuasion is all about convincing your potential customers of your point of view, influencing them to agree with you, or motivating them to take specific action, like buying your product or service. Here are some steps you can follow to improve your persuasion skills:

1. Understand Their Needs: The more you know about a person, the easier it will be to persuade them. Take time to understand your prospect's challenges, needs, and wants. This will enable you to position your offering as a solution more effectively.

2. Show Empathy: People are more likely to be persuaded by those who understand and share their feelings. Empathy helps you build a stronger emotional connection with your prospects.

3. Use Facts and Evidence: Support your arguments with data, statistics, and evidence. People are more likely to be persuaded when they know your point of view is not based on emotions alone but also backed by facts.

4. Stay Positive: Maintain a positive attitude throughout your conversation. This can make your prospects more receptive to your message and more likely to agree with you.

Subsection 6.4: Negotiation Skills: Closing Deals Like a Pro

Negotiation is a crucial part of outbound sales mastery. It's not just about convincing a potential client to buy your product; it's more about finding a common ground where both parties are satisfied. Here are some helpful tips for enhancing your negotiation skills:

1. Do Your Homework: Know about the industry, the prospect's company, and what they might value in your product. The more information you have, the better position you'll be in during negotiations.

2. Be Patient: Negotiations take time. Don't rush. Sometimes, merely being patient can lead the other party to reveal information or make concessions.

3. Know Your Walk-Away Point: Before entering into negotiations, know the minimum outcome you're willing to accept and stick to it.

4. Seek Win-Win Results: Aim for a solution that benefits both parties. This approach not only helps in closing the current deal but can also open doors for future business.

By mastering effective communication and negotiation skills, you can foster better relationships with your prospects and close more deals, turning ordinary conversations into profitable opportunities.

Section 7: Overcoming Obstacles and Objections in Sales

Subsection 7.1: The Art of Turning Objections into Opportunities

Overcoming objections is a major part of the sales journey. Those who master the ability to turn negatives into positives have substantial sway in influencing the outcomes of their sales engagements. Objections in sales are common and expected so let's see them as they are: opportunities for clarification, engagement improvement and relationship deepening.

Understanding the Concept of Sales Objections

A sales objection is a valid reason a prospect provides to refrain from completing a purchase. Oftentimes, these objections come across as challenges, beliefs, opinions, or specific problems that come up during the sales process. They can include concerns about pricing, product features, contractual terms, delivery times and the list goes on.

Objections can be a sign that the prospect has valid concerns, or they may simply be stalling due to internal uncertainties. Regardless of the motivation behind the objection, it's important to address it promptly, honestly, and assertively. This is where the art of turning objections into opportunities comes into play.

Recognizing Objections

Before you can overcome a sales objection, you must identify it. The trick here is understanding that objections typically take on two forms: explicit and implicit. Explicit objections are outright challenges to your offering or questions about its exact value. Implicit objections, on the other hand, are often subtle and take the approach of hesitations, doubts, or non-verbal cues demonstrating unease or uncertainty.

Transforming Objections Into Opportunities

Bypassing objections is not the answer. Listen to the customer's concerns, validate their feelings, and address said concerns proactively. Instead of just considering an objection as a roadblock, think of it as a possibility to deepen your understanding of your customer's needs and provide a solution tailored to those needs.

1. **Listen Carefully**: Active listening involves understanding the prospect's perspective, acknowledging their concerns, and responding to them contextually.
2. **Show Empathy and Understanding**: Put yourself in the prospect's shoes and understand their point of view. This creates a genuine connection and trust between you and the prospect.
3. **Ask Clarifying Questions**: Dig deeper into the objections to fully understand the root cause of their hesitation. By doing this, you can accurately address and potentially overturn the objection.
4. **Offer Solutions, Not Arguments**: Provide resolution to the objections, showing how your product or service meets their specific needs or resolves their challenges, instead of debating with the prospect.
5. **Follow Up**: Following up with the client ensures you maintain an open line of communication and shows your dedication to their satisfaction.

Remember, the ultimate goal is not merely getting the sale, but building a long-term relationship based on mutual trust, respect, and value creation.

Preparing for Future Objections

It's crucial to learn from every interaction and objection raised. Over time, you will start to notice patterns in the concerns that potential clients have about your offering. Use these patterns to anticipate objections and develop responses that will eliminate, or at least reduce, their impact.

This portion of the sales journey may sometimes be challenging but remember this: every obstacle overcome strengthens your sales skills and brings you one step closer to sales mastery. Each objection combated is not just a win, it's a lesson and an opportunity to grow more capable in your craft of outbound sales mastery.

Subsection 7.1: Understanding the Nature of Objections

Understand this, objections are not outright rejections. They are an expression of the clients' concerns, lack of clarity, or certain doubts regarding your products or services. Every objection poses a query and answering this helps the client understand the product further.

Recognize the Underlying Concern

Look beneath the overt objection. Most objections stem from the prospects fear and uncertainty. They might appear as complaints about your service or product, but in reality, it's their way of seeking assurance about the value your product promises.

Here's a trivial example. When a prospect says, "I find your product too expensive" this hides the question, "Is the high cost of your product justified? Will I get equivalent value out of this investment?". So instead of defending the price, convince them about the value they will get from the product.

Reiterate and Confirm

Once you understand the objection, repeat it back to the prospect to ensure you have it right. It could sound something like, "So, if I understand correctly, you're concerned about..." By restating the objection, you assure the prospect that their concerns have been noted and validates their worries.

Address the Objection

Post restating, answer the objection. This might require you to explain the functionality of your product/service, compare it with alternatives, or even provide testimonials from other clients. For instance, if they object to the price, explain how your product is superior to cheaper alternatives or how it provides more value for money in the long run.

When addressing objections, remember to stay respectful and empathetic. Treat these objections as genuine concerns rather than obstacles.

Validate the Resolution

Once you've addressed the objection, check if the prospect is satisfied with your response with a question like, "Does that address your concern?", "Is there anything more you'd like to understand?" or, "Have I answered your question clearly?". This interaction will not only assure the prospect of their decision but will also foster a stronger positive relationship between you and them.

Learning from Objections

Every objection you face is an opportunity to learn and improve. Understanding recurring objections can help you identify gaps in your products, clarify your sales pitch, or work on various aspects of your client interaction. Consider these objections as feedback and strive to solve them proactively for future endeavors. This mindset will not just help you overcome objections but also avoid them in the future.

Overcoming objections is a crucial part of any outbound sales process. It's not just about persuading a prospect, but also about building relationships that last. Embrace objections and make them your stepping stones towards successful selling. Remember, the power lies in understanding the core concerns, maintaining open communication, and crafting convincing responses. Above all, it's realizing that objections are opportunities for growth, for both you and your business.

Subsection: Tackling Objections Head-On: Proven Strategies and Practices

In the exciting world of outbound sales, dealing with customer objections is an essential part of the journey. Like fierce winds testing the resilience of a sailboat, these objections test the mettle of every salesperson. The knack of turning these objections into golden opportunities separates seasoned sales experts from novices. This subsection offers a comprehensive guide about handling objections head-on, elucidating proven strategies that can transform your sales process while fortifying your relationship with potential clients.

Understanding Sales Objections

Objections in sales are more than mere refusals; they provide crucial clues about the prospect's needs and reservations. Scrutinize them properly, and you might find yourselves with actionable insights to sway the decision in your favor. Understanding objections also demands empathy and patience, as customers often articulate their concerns immersed in fear, mistrust, or misunderstanding. Therefore, arm yourself with knowledge and empathy alike, to dig deeper into such reservations and gently guide the clients towards your offerings.

Different Types of Sales Objections

Sales objections can be understood within multiple contexts, but they broadly fall under four categories: Need-Based, Trust-Based, Money-Based, and Time-Based. As the names suggest, these objections arise out of a lack of perceived need, trust issues, financial constraints, or poor timing. Each one requires a unique approach and understanding to effectively navigate the conversation towards a win-win situation.

Strategies to Overcome Sales Objections

- **Active Listening**: The first step towards resolving objections is to genuinely listen. Only when you're aware of their concerns can you address them. By actively listening – responding appropriately and asking follow-up questions – you communicate empathy and sincerity, setting the foundation for constructive dialogue.

- **Empathize and Validate Concerns**: Step into the customer's shoes. Empathizing with their concerns and validating their feelings builds trust. Articulate your understanding of their situation before offering a solution. It shows the customer that they're heard, and you're committed to serving them, regardless of whether they make a purchase or not.
- **Solution-based Selling**: Once the customer's concerns are identified, transition towards offering solutions. If a prospect expresses Money-Based objections, offer flexible pricing plans or emphasise the value they will get for what they pay. A Time-Based objection can be tackled using product demonstrations that show how your product/service can save them time in the long run.
- **Proactively Address Objections**: Anticipate common objections and address them before they arise. This proactive approach not only saves time but also creates an impression of a consultative salesperson who's genuinely interested in helping the customer. Craft your sales pitch highlighting how your product addresses common reservations and see the trust with the prospects strengthen immensely.
- **Effectively Use Testimonials and Case Studies**: When dealing with Trust-Based objections, leverage social proof such as testimonials, case studies, or customer reviews. They showcase verifiable success stories with your product, tilt the scales in your favor, and instill a sense of confidence in hesitant prospects.
- **Always Follow Up**: The sales conversation shouldn't end at the objection. Be resilient. Show empathy, respect their decision, but also express your intent to follow up. Often, objections are raised when prospects need more time to process the information

or factors beyond your control. With time, these constraints may change, opening doors for fruitful future engagements.

Applying these strategies will not only lead to overcoming objections but also foster sustainable relationships that deliver long-term value. Remember, objections are not rejections. They're opportunities for you to showcase your resilience, empathy, and commitment to the client's successe, laying the groundwork for a deep-rooted, mutually beneficial association over time.

Chapter 15: Adapting a Growth Mindset: Key to Overcoming Sales Objections

In the ever-competitive world of outbound sales, objections from potential customers are not just probable; they're practically a rite of passage. Embracing from the onset that objections will arise can dramatically shift your perspective and enhance your ability to overcome these obstacles. In this chapter, we will explore a pivotal tool for any sales professional: adopting a growth mindset.

Unpack the Potential Objections

Before we navigate the seas of sales objections, it's crucial to outline what these objections typically look like. They can range from simple, dismissive objections ("I'm too busy right now.") to more concrete, consequential factors ("We don't have the budget for this product."). Recognizing the root cause behind these objections will equip you with the tools to turn a 'no' into a 'yes'.

The Power of a Growth Mindset

Shifting a potential customer's view from a hard 'no' to a promising 'yes' requires a shift within a salesperson first. Here is where the growth mindset comes into play. Defined by psychologist Carol Dweck, a growth mindset "is based on the belief that your basic qualities are things you can cultivate through your efforts" (Mindset, 2006).

An individual with a growth mindset sees challenges as opportunities for growth, perceives effort as a path to mastery, learns from criticism, and finds inspiration in others' success. In the context of outbound sales, this means viewing objections not as insurmountable roadblocks, but as a chance to learn, adapt, and grow.

Cultivating a Growth Mindset in Sales

Not everyone naturally possesses a growth mindset. However, it is possible and invaluable to instigate one. Here are some steps to cultivating this essential sales tool:

Embrace the Challenge

Start by reframing challenges as chances to grow. Whether a potential client gives a firm 'no' or is undecided, view this as an opportunity to adapt your selling method.

Practice Persistence

Sales is a game of resolve. The law of averages suggests that the more potential customers you interact with, the higher the probability of making a sale. Developing persistence enables you to go the extra mile and not give up easily.

Seek Feedback

Invite and accept feedback. Even the most experienced salespeople have room for improvement. Critique should be seen as a source of growth and not as an attack on your capabilities.

Celebrate Learning

Celebrate every bit of knowledge obtained from trial and failure. Each failed sale is an opportunity to tweak your approach and improve your skill.

In this growth-oriented frame of mind, sales objections become less of a frustration and more of a chance to build a bridge to a successful sale. By embracing a growth mindset, you can turn the perceived negatives of objections into actionable positives, potentially transforming your results and overall career in outbound sales.

Ensure you carry this mindset with you throughout your sales journey. It promises to be a powerful tool in overcoming sales objections, transforming most rejections from setbacks into steps towards sales mastery. Remember, in every objection, lies an opportunity for growth and learning.

7.1 Recognizing and Understanding Objections

As an outbound sales professional, it's crucial to anticipate that potential clients may have objections about your product or service. These objections are often a result of perceived risks, skepticism, misunderstanding, or a lack of information. They are not necessarily a reflection of your selling skills but part of the buyer's journey.

Understanding and effectively handling objections can make the difference between closing a sale and missing out on an opportunity. It's helpful to keep in mind that objections are not always a flat-out 'no'. Instead, they might be your prospect's way of requesting more information before they can make a decision or are ready to commit.

Types of Sales Objections

Broadly speaking, objections can be grouped into four categories: price, product, need, and timing.

- **Price:** These objections stem from your prospects' belief that your product or service is too expensive. This perception could stem from a lack of perceived value or a tight budget.
- **Product:** These objections are about the actual product or service. It can come in the form of skepticism about its functionality, performance, or quality.
- **Need:** In these cases, the prospect does not see the need for your product or service. They may feel they are already adequately equipped or don't see how your offer aligns with their goals or challenges.
- **Timing:** Often, prospects are satisfied with their current solution or are busy with other urgent matters, making them hesitant to invest time and resources into something new.

Recognizing the type of objection can guide your strategy to overcome it.

Overcoming Sales Objections

Overcoming objections involves a certain level of skill and experience. Here are a few strategies worth exploring:

- **Questioning:** If you're facing a price objection, for example, ask questions that can help uncover the prospect's underlying concerns. Instead of justifying the price from the get-go, try to understand what they see as a fair price and why.
- **Providing Evidence:** This might mean sharing testimonials from satisfied clients, case studies showcasing the product's effectiveness, or data that supports your claims, especially useful for product objections.
- **Demonstrating Value:** For need-based objections, focus on communicating the value your product or service can bring. Explain how it can address their challenges or contribute to their success. Use success stories that show how others have benefited to create relatability.
- **Creating Urgency:** When it comes to a timing objection, creating a sense of urgency can help to encourage a decision. Limited-time offers or explaining how delaying can lead to missed opportunities or unchanged challenges can influence the prospect's perspective.

However, always ensure that your response is respectful and understanding. A condescending or dismissive response can ruin the relationship.

The Art of Persistence

It is essential not to give up at the first objection. Just because a prospect has objections doesn't mean they aren't interested. Being persistent, respectfully pushing back, and probing deeper can often help you unearth the real concerns troubling your prospect.

Remember to practice active listening. Hear their objections, empathize with them, and respond thoughtfully. It can build trust and open the door for further dialogues that may eventually lead to a sale.

Ultimately, mastering the art of overcoming objections can significantly boost your outbound sales success. It's about building trust, proving value, and being prepared for any concerns your prospect might have.

By learning to look at objections as opportunities, you'll start to transform your approach, making you a more effective and empathetic salesperson, transforming not just your sales but your own personal growth journey as well.

Section 8: Scaling Your Sales and Transforming Your Business

Chapter 8.1: Enhancing Sales Efficiency through Automation

Sales automation is a brilliant strategy that businesses deploy to free up their sales team from mundane and repetitive tasks, allowing them to focus more time and effort on revenue-producing activities. Automating some of these tasks fosters a streamlined workflow that ensures every prospect is properly engaged, and no opportunity falls through the cracks.

8.1.1: Understanding Sales Automation

Sales automation is the process of leveraging tools, software, and technology to automate repetitive, time-consuming tasks associated with fundraising and sales process management. These tasks often involve follow-ups, sending emails, tracking possible leads, updating contact information, and documentation processes. By automating these tasks, your sales team can focus on the intricate and personal aspects of sales that build customer relationships and close deals.

8.1.2: Components of Automated Sales

A well-implemented automated sales process can have five key components:

- **Automated Emails:** This involves setting up automated rules that trigger based on different criteria, sending the right kind of content to different leads at the right time.
- **Contact, Deals, and Task Management:** Systems can automatically cleanse databases, manage-and-track deals, create tasks, and even assign them to the right team member based on predefined criteria.
- **Predictive Lead Scoring:** This system scores leads on their attractiveness and readiness to convert based on a plethora of data points and cues.

- **Sales Campaign Management:** Automation can manage multi-channel campaigns as well as send personalized messages to the potential customers.
- **Sales Analytics and Reporting:** An automated system can generate action-oriented analytics allowing sales teams to foresee trends and pivot when necessary.

8.1.3: Benefits of Sales Automation

Automation can drastically transform any sales department. Here are some game-changing benefits:

- **Saves Time:** Automation reduces the time spent on repetitive tasks and allows your sales team to focus on the core activity of selling.
- **Error Reduction:** By minimizing human intervention, the possibility of errors is greatly reduced.
- **Improved Customer Relationship Management:** CRM systems can automate follow-up reminders, lead tagging, email campaigns, and many others, making interaction with the customer seamless.
- **Scalability:** Automation allows businesses to scale their sales activity according to their business needs without considerable extra expenditure.
- **Data-Driven Decision Making:** Automated data compilation, analysis, and visualization can help make decisions that are based on real-time insights and customer behavior.

8.1.4: Sales Automation Tools to Consider

Several tools can help streamline and automate sales processes:

- **CRM Software:** Tools like Salesforce, Zoho, HubSpot, etc., provide robust automation capabilities across the sales funnel.
- **Email Marketing Tools:** Platforms such as Mailchimp and Constant Contact can be used to set up automated email sequences and manage large-scale outreach campaigns.
- **Social Media Management Tools:** Tools like Hootsuite and Buffer can automate, streamline and manage social media posting and engagement.

Sales automation should not be seen as a tool to replace a sales team but should be leveraged to assist them in higher-order sales tasks by cutting out redundant tasks. Integrating automation into sales operations is a giant leap toward outbound sales mastery and the transformation of your business. Let your sales automation journey start today.

Subsection: The Art of Efficient Scaling

In this crucial subsection of "Scaling Your Sales and Transforming Your Business," we will delve deep into the art of efficient scaling. Here, we'll explore the techniques, strategies, and philosophies that make the difference between a stagnant business and one that is continually evolving, growing, and succeeding.

Understanding What Scaling Means

Scaling is more than just growth. It's about growing your sales and your business efficiently. The idea is to increase your revenues exponentially while adding resources incrementally. Achieving this balance takes careful planning, strategic investment, and accurate tracking and measuring of performance.

The Relevance of Outbound Sales in Scaling

Outbound sales play a significant role in effective scaling. As your salespeople reach out and bring in more business, the resultant influx of customers and profit provides the momentum you need to scale up your operations.

Know your Market

In order to scale efficiently, you need to understand your market intimately. Use your market research, customer feedback, and sales data to recognize the real value you provide for your customers and leverage this knowledge in your sales pitches and marketing campaigns.

Set Clear Goals

Your scaling efforts should always be guided by clear, measurable goals. These could involve reaching a specific revenue target, expanding to new markets, or achieving a certain sales conversion rate. Clear goals provide direction and motivation for your entire team.

Streamline Your Operations

To scale efficiently, it's essential that you streamline your operations to minimize wasted time, effort, and resources. Optimize your sales processes, implement effective sales software, train your team, and automate tasks where possible. All of this leaves you better positioned to scale your sales without increasing your workload dramatically.

Training and Development

Your sales team is fundamental to your scaling efforts. On-going training and development ensure they have the skills necessary to close the increased volume of sales. Remember, as you scale your sales, your team should also scale their skills.

Analyze and Adapt

Scaling involves continuously analyzing your performance, identifying areas of improvement, and adapting your strategies accordingly. Monitor your sales figures, customer feedback, market trends, and competitors closely to stay ahead of the curve.

The Power of Networking and Partnerships

Form strategic partnerships and alliances to expedite the process of scaling. They not only bring in new business but also provide opportunities for learning, development, and industry insights.

Conclusion

Scaling is not just about growing your sales and business but doing it in a way that maximizes efficiency and profitability. It's about knowing your market, setting clear goals, streamlining operations, investing in your team, continually analyzing your performance, and leveraging the power of partnerships.

Remember, mastering the art of outbound sales is key to scaling efficiently and transforming not just your business, but your entire approach to entrepreneurship.

Subsection 8.1: Effective Strategies for Scaling Outbound Sales

When a business reaches a certain level of achievement in its outbound sales, the next logical step is to scale. This requires well-defined strategies that maintain the quality of sales while significantly increasing quantity. This process is crucial to your business progression and must be handled with precision and expertise.

Scaling outbound sales involves fine-tuning your sales model, improving efficiencies, re-evaluating your targets, and ensuring your sales team is up-to-date with the right skills.

Step 1: Fine-tuning Your Sales Model

If your organization is considering scaling its outbound sales, it means that your sales model has enjoyed some level of success. But business is about constant evolution, so it is always important to refine your current sales model to ensure your success is replicable on a larger scale. To fine-tune your sales model effectively, determine the key elements that contributed to the success of your sales, then seek to bolster these factors while mitigating any areas of weakness.

Step 2: Boosting Efficiencies

To scale effectively, your organization needs to perform sales tasks faster and better. This often involves maximizing the current resources or capabilities through automation or streamlined processes. Workflow tools, AI, chatbots, CRM systems, and other technology solutions can be used to simplify tasks and hasten your sales processes. By doing so, you could engage more leads without sacrificing the quality of customer interaction and thereby significantly augment outbound sales.

Step 3: Reassessing Your Target Market

Often during scaling, businesses need to reassess their target markets. As you plan to increase your sales volume, you must ensure that your audience pool is wide and deep enough to accommodate this expansion. Various market analysis tools such as SWOT and PESTEL can be used to get an in-depth understanding of market dynamics, audience scope, and potential for profitability in terms of scale.

Step 4: Upskilling Your Sales Team

No matter how efficient your strategies and technologies are, at the heart of every sales process is your sales team. To scale your sales effectively, your team must be equipped with the skills necessary to handle more complex demands and larger sales volumes. This can be achieved through regular training sessions, mentorship programs, and other developmental activities.

Once you effectively execute these steps, you'll be on track to take your business to unprecedented heights. However, remember that scaling is a continuous process and not a onetime event. It requires constant monitoring, adjustment, and improvement to maintain and increase success.

Choosing to scale your outbound sales marks an important milestone in your business journey, but it's just the beginning. With strategic planning, proactive actions, and consistent efforts, you can achieve your scaling goals and transform your business.

Remember, mastery is not an event but a journey. Keep investing in your knowledge, skills, and strategies. The market is kind to those who are prepared, relentless, and adaptive. Let your outbound sales mastery journey continue to inspire you, your team, and all whom your business serves.

Subsection 8.1: Establishing a Solid Resources Infrastructure for Outbound Sales Growth

As your outbound sales endeavors gather momentum, you'll quickly realize the importance of a solid infrastructure that enables consistent growth. Your outbound sales team must adhere to a framework that allows for scalability, as an unprepared approach to expansion could lead to disorganized efforts, missed sales opportunities, and ultimately, a stifled business transformation. This need leads us to a primary focus that plays a key role in scaling: establishing a robust resources infrastructure.

8.1.1 Assemble a Strong Sales Team

The backbone of your outbound sales drive lies within the team executing the mandate. Building a strong, experienced, and motivated sales team is essential for scalable growth. While focusing on gathering experienced salespeople, also strive to foster an environment that enables skill development, nurturing employees to transform into outbound sales experts. Recruitment initiatives should target high-potential candidates, preferably those with exceptional communication skills and a knack for establishing long-lasting customer relations.

8.1.2 Building a Resource-Rich Environment

Imbued with the requisite knowledge, your sales team needs resources to optimally perform their roles. Resources range from sales software tools, educational materials, customer relationship management (CRM) systems, meeting spaces, and more. Ensuring these resources are in place adds a crucial level of organization to sales operations, preventing undue downtime and hiccups in your sales process that could hinder scalability.

8.1.3: Investing in Technology

The modern sales climate heavily relies on technology for efficiency and accuracy. Look into integrating helpful tech tools such as CRM systems, predictive analytics software, and email tracking tools. These will streamline your sales processes, improve customer interactions, and provide useful data insights. Remember, technology investments must aim to simplify processes, not further complicate them.

8.1.4: Consistent Training Programs

Investing in regular training programs keeps your team up-to-date with the latest sales techniques, industry changes, and advancements in technology. A well-trained sales team capable of adapting to emerging trends will help maintain a high level of output as your sales efforts scale.

8.1.5: Robust Metrics System

Any growing outbound sales team needs a robust metrics system in place to monitor performance, isolate areas for improvement, and recognize top performers. By using KPIs like the number of leads generated, the conversion rate, and the CRM activity level, you can track progress and tweak strategies for increased productivity.

Understanding the importance of establishing a solid resources infrastructure is pivotal in the expansion of your outbound sales endeavors. With the right team, tools, tech, trainings, and tracking, you can initiate a sales model that consistently upholds a high level of performance and seamlessly adapts to increased demands. This not only enables scalable growth but drives the transformative change your business needs to dominate your industry sphere.

Subsection 8.1: Accelerating Growth through an Outbound Sales Strategy

It's undeniable: To transform your business and achieve fantastic growth, an effective outbound sales strategy is more than just a nice-to-have—it's utterly crucial. Let's delve into what outbound sales can do for your business and how to master it.

Why Outbound Sales Matters

Sales are the lifeblood of any business. They fuel growth and are responsible for transforming small ventures into Fortune 500 companies. Outbound Sales focuses on customer acquisition via proactive selling techniques such as cold calls, emails, and social selling. This method increases the growth potential of a company by reaching out to prospective clients who may not have discovered the company or its products or services.

Balancing Quality and Quantity in Leads

An efficient outbound sales strategy is about more than simply contacting as many leads as possible. It's about finding the right balance between quality and quantity of leads. A large number of leads may seem great, but if the quality is low, it will result to more rejection and wasted resources. Conversely, high quality leads that don't scale limit your growth potential.

Therefore, one of the key components of mastering outbound sales is establishing a sustainable strategy for generating high-quality leads on a large scale. An effective method includes identifying your ideal customer profile then using this to target and approach prospective clients in an appealing manner.

Building an Effective Outbound Sales Team

Another crucial aspect of outbound sales mastery involves building an efficient sales team. Here are some pertinent points:

- **Recruitment: ** The ideal sales representative understands your product/service, understands your market, and has a knack for engaging with people.

Look beyond immediate experience and focus on attitude and potential when recruiting.
- **Training: ** Invest in regular training to keep your sales team updated on product changes, market shifts, and the evolving buyer's journey. The training should instill the skills of effective story-telling, problem-solving, assertiveness and dealing with objections.
- **Motivation: ** Intrinsic and extrinsic motivation should be leveraged to keep the sales team determined, even in the face of rejections. Make good use of incentives, create a competitive yet friendly atmosphere, and recognize top performers to boost morale.
- **Tools: ** Provide your team with the right tools. The use of Customer Relationship Management systems (CRM), email scheduling tools, productivity apps, etc., can make them more organized and efficient.

Metrics, Analytics, and Continuous Improvement

Data analysis is the backbone of an effective outbound sales strategy. Keep track of critical metrics like conversion rates, email open rates, lead response time and customer acquisition cost. Use these metrics to analyze and optimize your sales performance continually. The goal is not only to track results but also to provide insights into how processes can be refined for better outcomes.

Building Customer Relationships

Lastly, remember that each sale is the beginning of a relationship. Engage in post-sale follow-ups, seek customer feedback, and maintain open channels of communication. Happy customers not only provide valuable reviews but can also lead to referrals, thus, driving more sales.

Remember, mastering outbound sales and scaling your business is not an overnight affair. It is about constantly evolving, learning, and striving for improvement. By understanding your target customers, building a powerhouse sales team, leveraging data, and nurturing customer relationships, you can transform your business and take it to unparalleled heights of success.

Section 9: Case Studies: Successful Implementation of Outbound Sales Strategies

Case Study 1: Smith Co.: From Struggling to Thriving through Strategic Outbound Sales Implementations

During the economic slowdown of 2015, Smith Co., a software start-up company, was facing a critical juncture. The software-as-a-service (SaaS) that the company was built upon was not engaging with the market as expected, and generating revenue was becoming increasingly challenging. However, instead of opting for dissolution, Smith Co. decided to revise its outbound sales strategies.

The management team recognized that they had some severe limitations in their outreach and messaging to potential customers and, after a thorough SWOT assessment, decided to redefine their approach by implementing new outbound strategies.

Analyzing the Existing Sales Funnel

Smith Co. started by mapping out their existing sales process in close detail. This allowed them to identify bottlenecks and areas where potential clients were dropping out of the sales funnel. It became apparent that their sales cycle was overly complicated, leading to slow decision-making and an increased rate of missed opportunities.

Implementing a Personalized Approach

The company then started developing a more personalized approach towards their prospective customers. Rather than sending out generic emails and making scripted sales calls, the sales team was trained to personalize their approach for each potential client. They invested considerable effort in understanding the specific needs of each prospective client organization and aimed to position their product as a solution to those unique needs.

Investing in Sales Enablement Tools

Next, Smith Co. invested in sales enablement tools to increase the productivity and efficiency of their outbound sales team. They implemented a CRM (Customer Relationship Management) system to better track and manage their relationships with prospective customers. The CRM allowed them to automate certain tasks like follow-up emails, freeing up the sales representatives' time to focus on more critical outreach activities.

Regular Training and Evaluation

To stay at the peak of outbound sales mastery, Smith Co. started a routine of regular check-ins and training. Each sales representative's performance metrics were carefully monitored, and additional one-on-one coaching was provided as required. This constant process of evaluation and retraining helped the team stay sharp and responsive to changing market dynamics.

Result of the Successful Implementation

The implementation of the new outbound sales strategies resulted in a substantial improvement in Smith Co.'s sales performance.

Within six months, the company doubled its rate of conversion from lead to customer. This success led to a significant increase in revenue and helped Smith Co. navigate through the challenging economic climate. Additionally, the outbound sales restructure inspired a new energy within the company, leading to increased employee satisfaction and lower turnover rates.

Smith Co.'s journey is a testament that businesses can transform through strategic outbound sales implementations. The case study demonstrates how a struggling business can thrive by reviving its sales strategies and focusing on continuous improvement and effective CRM use. By adopting a personalized approach to reach prospective clients and focusing on constant improvement, any business can increase its outbound sales.

It's important to delve deeper into these tried-and-true strategies, understand their mechanics, applicability, and how they were tailored to suit Smith Co.'s unique business needs. With this knowledge, any company can replicate the success Smith Co. experienced and cultivate a similar transformative experience.

Case Study 1: The ABC Corporation's Transformation with Tailored Outbound Sales Approaches

The ABC Corporation is a globally recognized software company that had been struggling with stagnant sales figures for several years. Recognizing that their existing sales strategizing efforts were failing to keep pace with the changing market dynamics, they decided to revamp their approach towards outbound sales. This subsection aims to narratively illustrate how the ABC Corporation utilized outbound sales strategies effectively to transform their business into a powerhouse of exponential growth and productivity.

The Challenge: Decelerating Sales and Lost Opportunities

By the start of 2018, ABC Corporation had been encountering a decreasing trend in their annual sales. Their sales teams were stretched thin, dedicating exhaustive efforts towards creating warm leads and comprehensive client databases. Yet, they faced increasing difficulties in closing deals. Customer interactions had become transactional, and the personal touch necessary to build long-lasting relationships was notably absent.

The Approach: Adopting a Strategic Outbound Sales Methodology

ABC Corporation sought to redefine its outbound sales strategies by honing in on three key aspects: clear sales communication, targeted prospecting, and ongoing training for sales teams.

1. *Clear Sales Communication*: The company began by refining its sales scripts, focusing heavily on education rather than persuasion. Sales scripts became more product-focused, highlighting the advantages and utility of their software products rather than bombarding prospects with calls-to-action.
2. *Targeted Prospecting*: Secondly, ABC Corporation employed strategic targeting and segmentation. They classified leads into sensitive categories based on size, industry, and conversion potential. This approach helped build personalized interactions and close deals more effectively.
3. *Sales Team Training*: The company also invested heavily in ongoing sales training. Extensive product knowledge was imparted to empower the sales force to handle diverse client queries and concerns confidently.

The Implementation: Realizing the Power of Tailored Outbound Sales

Upon implementing these strategies, ABC Corporation began to witness a promising rise in their prospect conversions. The sales teams found more success in driving interest and responses from calls, emails, and meetings. The approach of education over persuasion helped in building a trusted rapport with their prospects, assisting them in moving confidently through the conversion funnel. Also, the power of targeted prospecting played a significant role in serving relevant leads to the sales teams, thereby cutting down on time and resource wastage.

The Result: A Turnaround in Sales Figures and Client Relationships

By the end of 2018, ABC Corporation saw a 37% increase in their sales figures. More significantly, the quality of client relations improved, with a rise in repeat customers and an upswing in customer loyalty and satisfaction. Post-sale service became a streamlined process, fostering an environment of on-going rapport and feedback collection.

A Path Forward: Continuous Improvement and Adaptation

The success of ABC Corporation underlines the power of effective outbound sales strategies. However, the key to sustained success lies in the continual refinement of these strategies in the face of evolving market dynamics and customer preferences.

This case study succinctly captures the transformative power of outbound sales strategies when implemented with careful forethought and strategy, re-emphasizing that optimized sales communication, targeted prospecting, and constant sales team training are primary catalysts for enhancing sales performance and redefining customer relations.

Stay tuned for more case studies, which will offer insights into unique challenges and the differing approaches businesses had to take to successfully implement outbound sales strategies to transform their business fortunes.

Case Study 1: Reimagining Sales - A Digital Marketing Agency's Successful Outbound Sales Journey

A premier digital marketing agency (let's call them DigiPhenom) provides a perfect example of successfully harnessing the power of outbound sales to grow exponentially. DigiPhenom's clients range from small to medium-sized businesses across various industries. Despite having a limited budget and a small sales team, the agency achieved quantum growth in customer acquisition and revenue streams with calculated adjustments in its sales strategy.

Challenges Faced

DigiPhenom confronted a common obstacle hurdle: a lack of brand awareness due to a congested market and thin resources. Its sales team relied almost entirely on referrals and minor inbound marketing efforts, which led to inconsistent revenue generation. They lacked an efficient strategy and the necessary outbound sales mastery to prospect, initiate conversation, and drive growth.

Adopting the Outbound Second Strategy

Given the hurdles, DigiPhenom sought to implement an effective outbound sales strategy that was low-cost, systematic, and scalable. The agency started by first understanding the characteristics of their ideal customer – size, industry, and digital needs. Investment in a good Customer Relationship Management (CRM) system was made next to organize and streamline their sales process. Ability to follow up timely and create personalized communication channels with their potential clients was the key goal.

Re-sculpting Lead Generation & Prospecting

They strategized their prospecting process by using LinkedIn Sales Navigator coupled with email automation tools. By leveraging LinkedIn, the sales team was able to perform targeted prospecting, identifying ideal potential clients to reach out to. With email automation tools, they sent out personalized, engaging emails at scale.

Enhancing Sales Conversations

DigiPhenom understood the significance of opening a dialogue with potential customers. Therefore, they meticulously prepared scripts for cold calls and emails. This preparation included understanding the prospects' pain points and how DigiPhenom's solutions could help tackle them. The strategy was to demonstrate value and generate curiosity during these conversations. DigiPhenom also implemented a 'follow-up' policy to keep the prospects engaged and maintain open lines of communication.

Measuring Results and Iterating Strategy

The key to their outbound sales strategy was measuring results consistently. They used the data from their CRM to track the response rate, conversion rate, deals closed effectively gauging the success of their strategy.

Results and Impact

Post implementing the outbound sales strategy, DigiPhenom witnessed a significant increase in their customer database. Cold calling and targeted emails led to the expansion of their customer base beyond their geographical boundaries, allowing them to tap into new market segments and industries. The success stemmed from the ability to make informed decisions through valuable insights drawn from the consistent measurement and evaluation of data.

Conclusion

This case study emphasizes the transformational power of outbound sales when executed strategically and systematically. Through thorough research, personalized outreach, and meticulous tracking, DigiPhenom not only overcame its laid-back growth pattern but managed to transform its sales process into a vibrant engine for consistent revenue, making them a classic example of outbound sales mastery.

Subsection: Case Study: ABC Corporation – Delivering Value Ahead of Profits

Context

ABC Corporation is a mid-size software solutions provider, established a decade ago, whose mission is to engineer excellent technological solutions. Although they had a solid product range, their sales were stagnating. They found themselves to be continually dealing with the same customers, which resulted in minimal growth and seemed incapable of penetrating new markets significantly.

Problem

Given the highly competitive environment within their industry, ABC Corporation realized they needed a game-changing sales strategy to thrive and stay ahead. Their existing methods were predominantly inbound, depending almost entirely on clients reaching out to them. They realized they were too passive in their approach and missed out on potential sales.

Solution

In order to scale up their operations and take control of the market, ABC Corporation decided to adopt an aggressive outbound sales strategy. They started by restructuring their sales team, hiring highly skilled personnel proficient in cold calling, social selling, email prospecting, and designing well-scripted pitches. They established a sales development team dedicated to identifying and researching potential clients, as suggested in an earlier chapter of this book.

Implementation

ABC Corporation used a multi-pronged approach for their outbound sales strategy:

1. **Email Campaigns:** The sales team drafted personalized emails for prospects, emphasizing the unique selling points of their software solutions. They utilized sensible and ethical follow-up strategies to maintain the connection with potential customers.
2. **Cold Calling:** Favouring a 'warm' cold calling approach, they did background research on companies and tailored their pitch to address their specific needs and pain points.
3. **Social Selling:** The team was trained to use social platforms such as LinkedIn, not only to tap potential leads but also to establish themselves as thought leaders in their industry.
4. **Customer-centric Approach:** The team adopted a customer-first mind-set. They focused on providing

vigorous, individualized, and enduring solutions, instead of going for a hard sell.
5. **Pipeline Management:** They incorporated a CRM system to track contacts, schedule follow-ups, and analyze the effectiveness of their strategies.

Results

The results of ABC Corporation's outbound sales campaign were remarkable:

- 60% increase in leads within the first year
- 45% of these leads converted into successful sales, a conversion rate almost twice their previous rate
- 30% increase in overall revenue
- Significant growth in market share
- Gained several long-term clients who were 'won over' by the personalized approach towards their business needs

Lessons Learned

ABC Corporation's success story demonstrates that a robust outbound sales strategy, executed by a well-prepared team, can yield significant results. It underlines the importance of personalization, research, and a customer-focused mindset.

One of the key takeaways from this case is the shift from a profit-first to a value-first approach. ABC Corporation understood that profits are a by-product of delivering robust solutions and nurturing long-term relationships with customers.

This successful implementation of outbound sales strategies holds valuable insights for every sales team: agility and personalization are potent tools in outbound sales. By moving away from a 'one-size-fits-all' technique, companies can penetrate deeper into markets and see impressive results.

9.1 Case Study 1: XYZ Software Company

Our very first case study examining the successful implementation of outbound sales strategies takes us to 'XYZ Software Company'. This midsize B2B tech business has grown immensely thanks to its commitment to outbound sales mastery.

Prior to incorporating outbound sales practices, they relied heavily on inbound marketing channels like SEO, content marketing, and social media to generate leads. However, they realized they were missing out on a significant sector of the market that could be directly reached using outbound strategies.

9.1.1 Pre-Implementation: The Limitations

Before implementing outbound strategies, XYZ Software Company faced multiple challenges. With an over-reliance on inbound marketing, the company was merely reacting to customer inquiries rather than proactively seeking prospects.

The primary drawbacks included:

1. **Passive Business Generation**: Waiting for customers to make the first move meant missing out on potentially interested parties who weren't already familiar with XYZ Software Company.
2. **Slow Customer Acquisition**: Relying on customers to find the company through online channels resulted in a slower sales operations tempo.

3. **Inadequate Market Penetration**: Without aggressive strategies to seek opportunities, there were important markets the company could not reach.

9.1.2 The Transformation Process

Recognizing these issues, XYZ Software Company started the transition to outbound sales mastery with the following steps:

1. **Training Sales Representatives**: Every member of the sales team received rigorous training on outbound strategies, like cold calling, sending cold emails, and hosting webinars.
2. **Creating Targeted Client Profiles**: By identifying ideal clients and markets, the sales team could focus their efforts more effectively.
3. **Integrating Software Tools**: The team incorporated sales acceleration tools like CRM software, data analytics, and automated email outreach to streamline their processes.
4. **Investing in Market Research**: Market research helped the team better understand potential customers and how to tailor their communication strategies accordingly.

9.1.3 Results and Analysis

The results of implementing outbound sales strategies were significant:

1. **Boosted Lead Generation**: XYZ Software Company began generating 40% more leads on a monthly basis, driving the sales growth.
2. **Increased Conversion Rates**: The targeted approach led to improved dialogue with potential

customers, resulting in a 30% increase in conversion rates.
3. **Enhanced Market Penetration**: The proactive approach helped the company tap into markets previously out of reach, expanding their potential client base.

9.1.4 Lessons Learned

The XYZ Software Company's journey allowed the team to make crucial observations and learn valuable lessons about outbound sales:

1. **Quality Over Quantity**: A large number of leads mean very little when most are uninterested. Targeted outreach can improve overall conversion rates.
2. **Balancing Inbound and Outbound**: While outbound sales yielded impressive results, it's essential to maintain inbound strategies to ensure a broad, dynamic sales technique.
3. **Evolution**: Outbound sales is an evolving process that requires continuous improvements and adaptations to keep pace with market developments.

The success that XYZ Software Company found with outbound strategies is not unique - other businesses can implement similar approaches to succeed. It's about setting clear goals, investing in the right tools and training, and learning from each interaction with prospects. As the case proves, outbound sales mastery can truly transform lives and businesses.

Section 10: The Future Trends in Outbound Sales.

Subsection 10.1: The Influence of Technology on Outbound Sales

The future of outbound sales directly ties up with the rapidly evolving landscape of technology. In an age where businesses are driven by digitization, sales strategies need to adapt and evolve to stay ahead in the game.

AI and Machine Learning Paths

We are entering an era where Artificial Intelligence (AI) and machine learning are not just buzzwords, but powerful tools that can optimize outbound sales strategies. AI can analyze vast amounts of data more accurately and quickly than any human, offering valuable insights that can enhance our approach to leads and prospects.

AI-based CRM systems will predict what customers are likely to buy, when, and why, making it much easier for sales teams to sell. Machine learning, on the other hand, can help us understand our customers better by recognizing hidden patterns in their customer journey. We can leverage these insights to personalize our approach, thereby adding tremendous value to our outbound sales efforts.

In the future, more nuanced styles of AI technology, such as natural language processing, and customer conversation analysis, will become a standard element of business sales strategies.

Role of Big Data

Big Data analytics plays an instrumental role in providing meaningful ways to connect with potential customers. By analyzing customer behavior, preferences, and commonly faced challenges, sales agents can use this information to fine-tune their sales pitch, addressing the potential customer's pain points more intimately and efficiently. In addition, predictive analytics can also help in forecasting trends, allowing us to stay one step ahead and refine our outbound sales strategies accordingly.

Virtual Reality & Augmented Reality

Virtual Reality (VR) and Augmented Reality (AR) add an entirely new dimension to the sales experience. They allow us to offer vivid, immersive product demonstrations to customers, irrespective of their geographic location. It becomes possible to represent complex data graphically or engage in a virtual walkthrough of a product or service in real-time, providing a rich and differentiated customer experience.

Chatbots and other Automated Response Systems

Automated response systems, including chatbots and automated emails, are an effective way to collect user information or address basic queries around the clock. As these tools become more sophisticated and interactive, they will serve as the primary contact point for many outbound sales interactions.

Role of Social Proximity

Outbound sales are also looking at a future where the convergence of real and digital-world identities happens. Concepts like social proximity aim at utilizing digital footprints to build sales strategies. Finding common connections through social platforms and using it as a bridge to connect with potential leads has seen success rates in the recent past.

In summary, the future of outbound sales is exciting and holds a lot of promise. Embracing technology and its advancements will be crucial in transforming lives and businesses. We will be at the intersection of meeting evolved customer expectations while keeping the business's growth momentum steady, acknowledging that technology will drive this evolution.

Subsection 10.1: The Impact of AI and Big Data on Outbound Sales

In the evolving landscape of outbound sales, one cannot ignore the transformative impact of Artificial Intelligence (AI) and Big Data. These technologies are not just future trends, but demarcations of a new era in sales and marketing.

AI-powered sales tools can analyze huge amounts of data, providing insights that human salespersons may overlook. For instance, such tools can identify patterns in customer behavior, helping to predict which leads are likely to convert into sales. Machine learning algorithms allow these tools to continually improve their predictive abilities, increasing their utility over time.

Big Data is equally significant in reshaping outbound sales. Salespeople now command vast amounts of information about potential customers. We're not talking about just demographics, but also buying habits, preferences, and behavioral data that reveal nuanced insights. Salespeople equipped with detailed consumer profiles can form personalized pitching strategies that flow naturally into conversations with potential customers.

Yet, access to data alone is insufficient. Data interpretation is critical. Raw data must be converted into useful insights. Making sense of huge volumes of data can be overwhelming. And here's where Big Data tools come into play, analyzing and extracting valuable insights that salespeople can leverage towards their strategies.

Subsection 10.2: The Growing Importance of Social Selling

Social media has become a platform for much more than connecting with friends. It's been a game-changer for businesses, offering new avenues for them to reach and engage their target audience. Outbound sales strategies have accordingly evolved and now an emergent trend in this space is 'social selling'.

Initially used to find leads, social media platforms now support the entire sales cycle. Salespeople use social media to identify potential customers, engage with them, nurture relationships, and close deals. With social media advertising getting more targeted, it's possible to direct messaging to precisely those people who will find it most relevant.

Sales strategies for social media also need to address changing customer behavior. Today's customers increasingly seek authentic interactions. Hard sell tactics are less effective on social media. Instead, providing valuable content, engaging with followers, and building relationships yield better results. Recognizing the trend, sales professionals will need to hone their social media skills and integrate social selling effectively into their strategy.

Subsection 10.3: The Emergence of Sales Automation

Future outbound sales will be defined not by how much effort salespeople put into selling but by how smartly they work. Enter sales automation - yet another trend that is poised to revolutionize the landscape of outbound sales.

Sales automation tools are designed to automate repetitive tasks, freeing salespeople to focus on what matters most - selling. From lead generation, lead scoring, to tracking customer interactions and follow-ups, every aspect of the sales process can be automated.

These tools are more than mere time savers. They bring consistency to the sales process, increase efficiency, reduce chances of errors, and help in nurturing leads more effectively. Salespeople can follow up with the right leads at the right time, a level of precision that can make all the difference in achieving sales goals.

Automation also impacts customer experiences— an increasingly important factor in sales. A prompt response can be a differentiating factor for a business. Automation ensures that no lead is left unattended and each receives timely responses, improving overall customer experiences.

While these trends are poised to define the future of outbound sales, it's crucial to remember that the core of sales still resides in understanding customer needs and offering valuable solutions. Technology is an enabler, but ultimately, it's interpersonal skills and relationships that make a successful salesperson.

Subsection 10.1: AI (Artificial Intelligence) in Outbound Sales

A major disruption in outbound sales has been the growth of AI-based technologies. As companies adapt to the ever-changing landscape, sales teams are experimenting and implementing AI to qualify prospects, engage potential clients, and generate sales.

AI for Lead Generation and Management

The old model of sales required hours of sifting through mediocre prospects to finally land a couple of potential leads. This process was not just time-consuming, but also costly. AI-enabled tech solutions are revolutionizing lead generation and management with their ability to scan massive databases and record online behavior quickly, which can be especially useful in B2B sales. Now, sales teams can cast a wider net and only dedicate time to conversations with high-potential prospects.

AI for Sales Conversation Intelligence

AI's implementation in sales doesn't stop at acquiring leads: it's also a powerful tool during the sales process.

Conversation intelligence is an AI-driven function that can offer in-depth analytics and actionable insights into the efforts of sales teams. With AI, you'll be able to identify trends and patterns, learn what language and strategies are the most effective, and come up with accurate predictions and forecasts to guide your future efforts.

AI for Personalization

AI helps to achieve more personal engagement with customers. It enables you to personalize content and offers based on predictive analytics. AI has the potential to learn from past behavior and craft personalized messages that resonate more effectively with customers at different levels within the buyer's journey.

AI for Sales Automation

Automation has a huge role in the future of outbound sales. A lot of the mundane, time-consuming sales tasks like sending emails, scheduling, and following up can be automated with intelligent sales software. AI-based tools can extend beyond automation by providing salespeople with suggested responses, next steps based on the customer's behavior, and even automated reasoning on the promises and risks of a transaction.

The Challenge with AI in Sales

As promising as the prospects of AI in sales are, there are significant challenges to its adoption. For instance, like any technology, AI is prone to errors and biases. It also requires significant investment in staff training, hardware, and software as well as an ability to blend the new technology with current systems and processes.

Nevertheless, AI's long-term benefits in efficiency, accuracy and costs far outweigh short-term challenges. As we move forward, companies that fail to adapt to these breakthroughs in outbound sales risk becoming obsolete.

In conclusion, the future of outbound sales offers an exciting fusion point for human intuition and artificial intelligence. In the subsequent subsections, we explore other trends shaping the future of outbound sales, such as the increasing importance of social selling and the dominance of mobile technology.

We will delve deep into the interplay of these trends, with the aim to equip the reader with enough insights to anticipate the outbound sales landscape in the future and make informed, strategic, and sustainable decisions.

Subsection 10.1: Predictive Selling – Leveraging AI and Machine Learning

As we move towards the future, outbound sales will no longer depend purely on human judgement and traditional strategies. In fact, we are already seeing significant progress in the use of artificial intelligence (AI) and machine learning in the field of sales. These technologies, due to their potential to analyze large volumes of data and derive meaningful insights, are going to be a game-changer in outbound sales.

AI-Powered Prospecting

AI has proven to be extremely effective in the initial stages of outbound sales, which involve identifying prospective clients and reaching out to them. Currently, salespeople often spend countless hours manually searching through online data and social platforms to find potential customers. AI can automate this process, using algorithms to scan online information and identify prospective clients based on specific criteria. This not only speeds up the process but also creates more accurate prospect lists.

Personalized Messaging with Machine Learning

Personalization is crucial in outbound sales. The more relevant your message is to a specific prospect, the more likely they are to engage. Here, machine learning offers an advantageous edge. It can analyze data from multiple sources such as past interactions, social media activities, and browsing patterns to create a comprehensive profile of a client's needs and interests. This in-depth analysis then enables sales teams to craft highly personalized messages, drastically increasing response rates.

Automated Follow-ups and Scheduling

AI can also help in scheduling and follow-ups, saving considerable time for sales professionals. Modern AI tools can automate follow-up emails, set up meetings, and even manage the calendar of sales representatives. This allows sales professionals to focus more on closing deals rather than logistical tasks.

Predictive Analytics for Sales Forecasting

Sales forecasting has always been a challenging part of outbound sales. However, with predictive analytics, an offshoot of AI, it becomes considerably easier and more accurate. Predictive analytics uses historical data and machine learning algorithms to make forecasts about future sales trends. This includes predicting which leads are most likely to convert, enabling sales teams to focus their efforts more strategically.

Enhancing Training and Sales Performance

Finally, AI and machine learning can also play a key role in training and improving the efficiency of sales professionals. AI tools can analyze performance data to identify the strengths and weaknesses of each salesperson. This insight can then be used to provide personalized training and support to help them improve their skills and tactics.

In conclusion, outbound sales are transitioning from a process that is predominantly manual and intuition-driven towards a more data-driven, automated field that leverages cutting-edge technologies like AI and machine learning. As technology continues to advance, we are likely to see even more integration of AI into outbound sales, completely redefining the industry. Those who can adapt and harness the power of these technologies will definitely stand out in the competitive world of outbound sales.

Subsection 10.1: The Rise of Automation and AI in Outbound Sales

As we take a glimpse into the future of outbound sales, we cannot avoid discussing the significant role of Artificial Intelligence (AI) and automation systems. Although some still think of these technological advancements as intimidating, their influence in the industry is undeniable and, when used properly, they can have substantial and positive effects on outbound sales strategies.

AI and Automation: The Game Changers

The first aspect to understand about AI and automation is that they are not designed to replace salespeople, but to improve their productivity and efficiency. AI technology, with its machine learning algorithms and predictive analysis capacities, can help salespeople sift through vast amounts of data, recognize patterns and provide actionable insights.

Automation tools, on the other hand, can handle repetitive and tedious tasks that often eat into a salesperson's valuable time. By automating tasks like lead generation, lead scoring, and follow-ups, salespeople can focus more on developing personal relationships with potential clients, crafting customized approaches, and closing deals.

Understanding Customer Behavior Through AI

AI's capability to process vast amounts of data and make sense of complex patterns makes it an ideal tool for understanding customer behavior. With AI, businesses can track a potential customer's digital footprint, understand their needs and preferences, and predict future behavior. Insights provided by AI can help sales teams strategically plan their outreach – knowing exactly when to approach a customer, what to offer them, and how to effectively communicate with them.

Boosting Personalization with AI and Automation

In an era where customers appreciate – and increasingly expect – personalized experiences, AI can drastically enhance the performance of outbound sales teams. It can help teams segment their customers, craft highly personalized messages, and guide one-on-one conversations. Moreover, with automation tools, personalized messages can be sent out systematically and consistently, ensuring that no potential customer falls through the cracks.

AI and Predictive Analytics: Streamlining the Sales Process

Another potential trend we're seeing within the outbound sales landscape is the use of predictive analytics powered by AI. This includes predicting which leads are likely to convert, what products they are likely to buy, and when they are likely to make a purchase. It significantly reduces guesswork and helps salespeople make data-driven decisions.

AI Chatbots and Virtual Assistants

AI Chatbots and Virtual Assistants are another important part of the future of outbound sales. They can interact with customers 24/7, answer their questions, process their orders, and even help them resolve problems. While they can't replace human interaction completely, they can take over for initial interactions and simple queries, freeing up time for sales personnel to interact with prospects on a deeper level.

Extracting Value from Big Data

As we accumulate more and more data, businesses will face the challenge of actually using this data effectively. AI and automation technologies will provide the key to unlocking the value hidden in this data. From predicting the best leads to understanding global market trends, big data combined with these technologies offers untapped potential for the outbound sales process.

The Ethical Considerations of AI

Despite the many advantages offered by AI and automation, it's essential to address the ethical considerations surrounding their use. Ensuring privacy, managing potential biases in AI algorithms, and providing transparency in AI-powered decisions are areas that will need ongoing attention.

In conclusion, the future of outbound sales will be significantly shaped by AI and automation technology. Embracing these advancements, adapting to their potential and understanding their limitations, will be a vital part of mastering outbound sales in the future.

Copyrights and Content Disclaimers:

AI-Assisted Content Disclaimer:
The content of this book has been generated with the assistance of artificial intelligence (AI) language models like CHatGPT and Llama. While efforts have been made to ensure the accuracy and relevance of the information provided, the author and publisher make no warranties or guarantees regarding the completeness, reliability, or suitability of the content for any specific purpose. The AI-generated content may contain errors, inaccuracies, or outdated information, and readers should exercise caution and independently verify any information before relying on it. The author and publisher shall not be held responsible for any consequences arising from the use of or reliance on the AI-generated content in this book.

General Disclaimer:
We use content-generating tools for creating this book and source a large amount of the material from text-generation tools. We make financial material and data available through our Services. In order to do so we rely on a variety of sources to gather this information. We believe these to be reliable, credible, and accurate sources. However, there may be times when the information is incorrect.
WE MAKE NO CLAIMS OR REPRESENTATIONS AS TO THE ACCURACY, COMPLETENESS, OR TRUTH OF ANY MATERIAL CONTAINED ON OUR book. NOR WILL WE BE LIABLE FOR ANY ERRORS INACCURACIES OR OMISSIONS, AND SPECIFICALLY DISCLAIMS ANY IMPLIED WARRANTIES OR MERCHANTABILITY OR FITNESS FOR ANY PARTICULAR PURPOSE AND SHALL IN NO EVENT BE LIABLE FOR ANY LOSS OF PROFIT OR ANY OTHER COMMERCIAL OR PROPERTY DAMAGE, INCLUDING BUT NOT LIMITED TO SPECIAL, INCIDENTAL, CONSEQUENTIAL, OR OTHER DAMAGES; OR FOR

DELAYS IN THE CONTENT OR TRANSMISSION OF THE DATA
ON OUR book, OR THAT THE BOOK WILL ALWAYS BE
AVAILABLE.

In addition to the above, it is important to note that language
models like ChatGPT are based on deep learning techniques
and have been trained on vast amounts of text data to generate
human-like text. This text data includes a variety of sources
such as books, articles, websites, and much more. This training
process allows the model to learn patterns and relationships
within the text and generate outputs that are coherent and
contextually appropriate.

Language models like ChatGPT can be used in a variety of
applications, including but not limited to, customer service,
content creation, and language translation. In customer
service, for example, language models can be used to answer
customer inquiries quickly and accurately, freeing up human
agents to handle more complex tasks. In content creation,
language models can be used to generate articles, summaries,
and captions, saving time and effort for content creators. In
language translation, language models can assist in translating
text from one language to another with high accuracy, helping
to break down language barriers.

It's important to keep in mind, however, that while language
models have made great strides in generating human-like text,
they are not perfect. There are still limitations to the model's
understanding of the context and meaning of the text, and it
may generate outputs that are incorrect or offensive. As such,
it's important to use language models with caution and always
verify the accuracy of the outputs generated by the model.

Financial Disclaimer

This book is dedicated to helping you understand the world of
online investing, removing any fears you may have about

getting started and helping you choose good investments. Our goal is to help you take control of your financial well-being by delivering a solid financial education and responsible investing strategies. However, the information contained on this book and in our services is for general information and educational purposes only. It is not intended as a substitute for legal, commercial and/or financial advice from a licensed professional. The business of online investing is a complicated matter that requires serious financial due diligence for each investment in order to be successful. You are strongly advised to seek the services of qualified, competent professionals prior to engaging in any investment that may impact you finances. This information is provided by this book, including how it was made, collectively referred to as the "Services."

Be Careful With Your Money. Only use strategies that you both understand the potential risks of and are comfortable taking. It is your responsibility to invest wisely and to safeguard your personal and financial information.

We believe we have a great community of investors looking to achieve and help each other achieve financial success through investing. Accordingly we encourage people to comment on our blog and possibly in the future our forum. Many people will contribute in this matter, however, there will be times when people provide misleading, deceptive or incorrect information, unintentionally or otherwise.

You should NEVER rely upon any information or opinions you read on this book, or any book that we may link to. The information you read here and in our services should be used as a launching point for your OWN RESEARCH into various companies and investing strategies so that you can make an informed decision about where and how to invest your money.

WE DO NOT GUARANTEE THE VERACITY, RELIABILITY OR COMPLETENESS OF ANY INFORMATION PROVIDED IN THE COMMENTS, FORUM OR OTHER PUBLIC AREAS OF THE book OR IN ANY HYPERLINK APPEARING ON OUR book.

Our Services are provided to help you to understand how to make good investment and personal financial decisions for yourself. You are solely responsible for the investment decisions you make. We will not be responsible for any errors or omissions on the book including in articles or postings, for hyperlinks embedded in messages, or for any results obtained from the use of such information. Nor, will we be liable for any loss or damage, including consequential damages, if any, caused by a reader's reliance on any information obtained through the use of our Services. Please do not use our book If you do not accept self-responsibility for your actions.

The U.S. Securities and Exchange Commission, (SEC), has published additional information on Cyberfraud to help you recognize and combat it effectively. You can also get additional help about online investment schemes and how to avoid them at the following books:http://www.sec.gov and http://www.finra.org, and http://www.nasaa.org these are each organizations set-up to help protect online investors.

If you choose ignore our advice and do not do independent research of the various industries, companies, and stocks, you intend to invest in and rely solely on information, "tips," or opinions found on our book – you agree that you have made a conscious, personal decision of your own free will and will not try to hold us responsible for the results thereof under any circumstance. The Services offered herein is not for the purpose of acting as your personal investment advisor. We do not know all the relevant facts about you and/or your individual needs, and we do not represent or claim that any of our Services are suitable for your needs. You should seek a registered investment advisor if you are looking for personalized advice.

Links to Other Sites. You will also be able to link to other books from time to time, through our Site. We do not have any control over the content or actions of the books we link to and will not be liable for anything that occurs in connection with the use of such books. The inclusion of any links, unless otherwise expressly stated, should not be seen as an endorsement or recommendation of that book or the views expressed therein. You, and only you, are responsible for doing your own due diligence on any book prior to doing any business with them.

Liability Disclaimers and Limitations: Under no circumstances, including but not limited to negligence, will we, nor our partners if any, or any of our affiliates, be held responsible or liable, directly or indirectly, for any loss or damage, whatsoever arising out of, or in connection with, the use of our Services, including without limitation, direct, indirect, consequential, unexpected, special, exemplary or other damages that may result, including but not limited to economic loss, injury, illness or death or any other type of loss or damage, or unexpected or adverse reactions to suggestions contained herein or otherwise caused or alleged to have been caused to you in connection with your use of any advice, goods or services you receive on the Site, regardless of the source, or any other book that you may have visited via links from our book, even if advised of the possibility of such damages.

Applicable law may not allow the limitation or exclusion of liability or incidental or consequential damages (including but not limited to lost data), so the above limitation or exclusion may not apply to you. However, in no event shall the total liability to you by us for all damages, losses, and causes of action (whether in contract, tort, or otherwise) exceed the amount paid by you to us, if any, for the use of our Services, if any. And by using our Site you expressly agree not to try to hold us liable for any consequences that result based on your use of our Services or the information provided therein, at any time, or for any reason, regardless of the circumstances.

Specific Results Disclaimer. We are dedicated to helping you take control of your financial well-being through education and investment. We provide strategies, opinions, resources and other Services that are specifically designed to cut through the noise and hype to help you make better personal finance and investment decisions. However, there is no way to guarantee any strategy or technique to be 100% effective, as results will vary by individual, and the effort and commitment they make toward achieving their goal. And, unfortunately we don't know you. Therefore, in using and/or purchasing our services you expressly agree that the results you receive from the use of those Services are solely up to you. In addition, you also expressly agree that all risks of use and any consequences of such use shall be borne exclusively by you. And that you will not to try to hold us liable at any time, or for any reason, regardless of the circumstances.

As stipulated by law, we can not and do not make any guarantees about your ability to achieve any particular results by using any Service purchased through our book. Nothing on this page, our book, or any of our services is a promise or guarantee of results, including that you will make any particular amount of money or, any money at all, you also understand, that all investments come with some risk and you may actually lose money while investing. Accordingly, any results stated on our book, in the form of testimonials, case studies or otherwise are illustrative of concepts only and should not be considered average results, or promises for actual or future performance.

tolerance, and the ability to consistently apply the strategies and techniques discussed.

Copyright Notice: All rights reserved. No part of this publication may be reproduced, distributed, or transmitted in any form or by any means, including photocopying, recording, or other electronic or mechanical methods, without the prior written permission of the publisher, except in the case of brief quotations embodied in critical reviews and certain other noncommercial uses permitted by copyright law.

www.ingramcontent.com/pod-product-compliance
Lightning Source LLC
Chambersburg PA
CBHW070943260726

48661CB00003B/1098